Babies
for
Burning

Babies for Burning

**Michael Litchfield
and Susan Kentish**

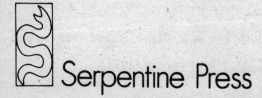

Serpentine Press

Printed and published by Serpentine Press Ltd., 21 Conduit
Street, London W1R 9IB.

ISBN 0 903961 024 (Paperback)

ISBN 0 903961 032 (Hardback)

To all the unborn babies who will be deprived of the opportunity of reading this book, or any other book, and to everyone, everywhere, who holds dear the principle of the sanctity of life for all human beings, whatever age and whatever size, however strong and however weak.

Contents

Section 6: **The Foreign Scene**

The Baby-snatchers

Conclusion

Appendices

Acknowledgements

The authors wish to thank all those who helped in an advisory capacity with this book, especially politicians, doctors, members of various voluntary organisations, and the editorial team of Serpentine Press Limited.

Introduction

It was in November, 1973, that we set out to research the working of the 1967 Abortion Act. The only limitation we imposed on ourselves was that the inquiry should be confined to the private sector, where most terminations are carried out, which meant that we would be excluding the National Health abortion service.

Some three years earlier, the Mrs. Justice Lane Committee, a Government-appointed body, had embarked on a similar project. The Lane Report is now comic history. Our findings and those of Lane could not be more diametrically opposed. Therefore, "Babies For Burning", is offered as an alternative to Lane.

We had no preconceived notions. Neither of us belonged — or do so now — to any lobby or pressure group on the subject. Sue, if anything, leaned towards the pro-abortion camp. Michael had not given the subject even a cursory glance. It was a topic that had not infringed our respective worlds. Nor was it a subject that, at the outset, was in any way destined to raise the barometer of emotion. We approached our task dispassionately, in complete isolation and detachment.

Michael had never heard of the Society for the Protection of Unborn Children. Susan did know of its existence, but had no specific knowledge of its aims and motivations. Certainly, none of the officials or members of that society were known to us.

Neither had we any connection with the Abortion Law Reform Society. During our research, we had no contact with either of the two antagonist organisations. We steered straight down the middle.

Every quote we reproduce was tape-recorded by us. Every document we refer to, we have kept for posterity.

Every fact we state, we can prove. We arrived at clinics unannounced, unheralded, without anyone knowing our true identity. We were always posing as a couple — sometimes married, sometimes single, sometimes one of us married to someone else and the other single — bargain-hunting around the abortion supermarkets.

Conversely, the Lane Committee forwarned all clinics, well in advance, of their impending "inspection".

Susan was given a pregnancy test by her own doctor before we started "shopping" for abortions. The test was negative. An eminent gynaecologist examined her internally. The result? "She was not pregnant and she had never been pregnant." Yet when Susan was examined internally by gynaecologists functioning in the private sector of the abortion market, and when she had urine samples tested, she was found, on every occasion, to be VERY MUCH PREGNANT.

So we went to the reputable gynaecologist at the end of the investigation for a final and thorough internal examination for Susan. His verdict was absolute: "Not pregnant, never has been pregnant, and no abnormalities that could possibly have led a trained doctor of any standing to diagnose pregnancy."

Every one of these gynaecologists was prepared to perform an abortion on Susan, a woman who was not even pregnant. Payment had to be by cash — in advance. Cheques were hardly ever acceptable.

We started our research where most girls begin when they discover themselves pregnant against their wishes — the pregnancy advisory and testing centres. There may be a certain prolixity about some of the chapters, but we felt it better to give direct dialogue, unexpurgated by us, so that the language has a certain living, stained and creased quality. This way, you are treated to the authentic anatomy and atmosphere of the abortion circus.

Section 1: Pregnancy Testing and Advisory Services

A Dark Alley

New Bond Street, London, is world-famous as a shopper's playground. Expensive furs, more expensive jewellery, trendy men's clothes, contemporary furniture and priceless antiques adorn the sophisticated shop windows: everything ancient and modern, artistic or functional, the aesthetic and the arid. Just a few hundred yards away is the roar of Oxford Street, the mecca of the big store moguls.

It would be possible to have worked in New Bond Street all one's life without knowing of the existence of Lancashire Court. This little court, which runs like a pipeline from New Bond Street, is really nothing more than a dingy, dank and rather fusty alley. There is a cluster of public telephone kiosks, where, after dark, the occasional tart can be seen touting for business in the glow of the lamplights. There is a constant aroma wafting from the kitchens of nearby restaurants.

It is to this squalid piece of London that many young women go when they are "shopping" for abortion bargains. They slip furtively from the flow of New Bond Street's pedestrian traffic and press the bell marked, "London Nursing Homes Ltd.", alongside a locked, shabby door of rather dreary-looking premises.

We followed the same route, pressed the same bell, and heard the same husky, female voice ask, through the intercom, what we wanted. We said that we had come in response to an advertisement in the London "Evening Standard" newspaper, offering pregnancy testing. The door opened automatically, by remote control, and we followed the narrow, creaking staircase to the first floor, as instructed.

"Reception" was a claustrophobic, diminutive room

containing one desk and a couple of chairs. A young woman, who we later discovered was called Sue Maxwell, was sitting behind the desk. She wore a white medical gown and National Health-styled, wiry spectacles. She interrupted her conversation with a coloured woman to tell us to go into an adjoining room, where she would talk to us later.

This room was more spacious, resembling a doctor's or dentist's waiting salon in a middle-class suburb. There were the usual glossy magazines, pamphlets on every conceivable facet of contraception, grey, metallic filing cabinets, "comfy" chairs, an executive desk and posters on the wall warning men — depicted rather as the enemy — to be more careful about which holes they crept into at night.

We were alone for about ten minutes before Mrs. Maxwell came and drew up a chair beside us. She was a lean, untidy and rakish woman in her twenties, looking painfully drained and pallid, almost as if her husband denied her sleep every night.

She asked for our names and addresses. We gave false ones. There was no attempt to ascertain whether we were telling the truth. We discovered very quickly that most people along the "pregnancy termination" conveyor belt — to use *their* euphemism — accepted that they would never really know the true identity of the women they were feeding to the abortion factories.

Mrs. Maxwell was also very interested to know how we learned about her agency. "We like to see how our advertising is going," she laughed. That nauseating laugh, virtually a sneer, of a kind we encountered countless times, was recorded for posterity on our tape-recorder, which was concealed in Sue Kentish's handbag.

A sample of Sue Kentish's urine was taken away for testing and a few minutes later Mrs. Maxwell returned, declaring, with a smile: "Sorry. Yes, that's positive." Then, she laughed again, which she might well have done considering Sue Kentish was *not* and *never* had been pregnant.

We asked if she could help us in any way. We did not mention abortion. They advertise themselves as a pregnancy testing and advisory service. So we asked for advice, and

Mrs. Maxwell's immediate response was: "Yes, certainly. You don't want a baby now?"

We confirmed that we did not and she asked us to follow her into the smaller room, where we sat around her desk. This is how the dialogue went:

Kentish: "Do you mind if I smoke?"

Maxwell: "No, not at all. I'll join you in a minute."

Mrs. Maxwell took out some papers from her desk and studied them for a few seconds.

Mrs. Maxwell: "What I can do is give you the details. The only thing I can't guarantee tonight is the date, the actual date of the appointment. I suppose you want it as early as possible?"

Already she was making guarantees and promises, although we had not even seen a doctor, and no reason for wanting an abortion had been offered or asked for. Abortion in Britain is still illegal unless it is performed for a valid reason under the Act. It is the duty of everyone offering advice or help with abortion to ensure that every case is fully investigated before condemning a living and thriving foetus to the incinerator. Legalised, it is a filthy enough trade, without it being further prostituted by a casual attitude that reduces unborn children to the status of jelly babies.

Mrs. Maxwell: "If you do want to have children later on, the operation doesn't prevent you from conceiving at all. You could tend to be more fertile."

Now she is really selling it...

Litchfield: "We are married and we don't want children at the moment."

Mrs. Maxwell: "Yes, sure, I understand that. The same as me." She laughed again, this time very heartily, as she wiped her nose with her fingers. There was something so weak and insipid, and yet so soiled about her that it made us both shiver mentally.

Litchfield: "It would rather impair our social life and everything." This was the ultimate in bait. It seemed impossible for any human being to hear such a scandalous remark and not to throw us out instantly into the rain. We, in the crudest possible terms, were making it clear that our social calendar was more important than a human life. Can you think of anything more offensive to normal thinking, caring, compassionate people? We leant over backwards to project the image of a reasonably affluent couple with all the material facilities to offer a child, and no mental hang-ups or problems that might give us grounds under the Act. We were saying: "We just don't want a kid. We have no reason for an abortion, but that is what we want and what can you do about it?"

Maxwell: "Yes, sure. So you've thought about it pretty well?"

Litchfield: "So long as there is not going to be a problem and it can be done."

Maxwell: "No, no, I wouldn't think so."

Kentish: "How much is it likely to cost?"

Maxwell: "I'm not too sure. It could be £80 or £100. It won't be any more than £100. But it would be wise to take £100 with you, to be sure. And for the following year, we will look after you for contraceptives. Anything like that, you don't have to pay for. Any advice, any gynaecological problems at all, any cancer smears, anything like that. We've got a Harley Street specialist who comes here. We don't charge you the usual £3.50 annual fee. Nothing. Usually people who become regular members here pay £3.50, plus the cost of pills and smears. No, you don't have to worry about that. And he's a very good doctor. Really good."

Litchfield: "It will be done at a good place?"

Maxwell: "Yes, very good. And, anyway, you'll be seen by two gynaecologists when you go there and you'll have a consultation with them and they'll make a final decision. It's not within my power to say everything will be okay, but I can say that you should go prepared for the operation the same day."

Kentish: "On what basis might they not do it?"

Maxwell: "Well, um... if you're married... um... there's four different clauses... um... probably that... um... I'll get the form and show you..." She left the room to fetch a copy of the official green abortion form.

Maxwell: "They could put it under clause two... that's

injury to physical or mental health of the pregnant mother. It could be. I don't know which one they will use. But probably that one, I'd imagine. It's quite legal, you know. There's no worries about it."

Litchfield: "Is it better for us to say the reason why we want it done or..."

Maxwell, interrupting: "He'll probably ask you, and if you just say that you don't want a child, well, they're very good, they really are. If you don't want to have a child at all, that's good enough for them. And they'll sort of help you with one of the reasons. I don't know which clause they would use."

Litchfield: "I was just worried whether being married would..."

Maxwell: "No, no, if you went to your GP and tried to get an abortion through the National Health, it would probably make a great deal of difference. And not only that, you would probably have to wait so long. We have had people ring up who have had to wait four or five weeks sometimes."

Kentish: "How long will I have to wait?"

Maxwell: "Well, in your case, next Monday, or I could probably guarantee Tuesday." She referred to a large diary. "I'm not sure about Monday. If you wanted it done over the weekend, it could probably be arranged, but I wouldn't know this until tomorrow."

Litchfield: "Where will it be done?"

Maxwell: "It's in Langham Street, actually. There used to be a clinic there, but it was closed down a while ago. Usually people are quite horrified when you mention Langham Street." This was yet another cue for her to evaporate into laughter. "It's the London Private Nursing Home. You have your own private room, your own telephone, visiting hours and they're really nice round there. You're very well looked after. You go there to see the gynaecologist and he'll do it the same day. And you'll have an overnight stay and you come out the next morning at about 8.30 or 9. You'll be fine. You must go prepared. Take all your overnight things and fast from the night before... from midnight. However, I'll give you one of these cards to take with you. You will find all the details there."

Litchfield: "Shall I take the money along when we go?"

Maxwell: "Yes, and they like it in cash." This was followed by great guffaws of merriment. "They used to take cheques, but so many of them bounced that they made it policy not to accept them any more."

Litchfield: "There is no risk, is there, in an operation at this stage?"

Maxwell: "No... no."

This is untrue. There is an inherent risk in all surgery when general anaesthetic is administered.

Litchfield: "What's the latest it can be done through you?"

Maxwell: "Twenty-two weeks."

Litchfield: "So she's well within the limit?"

Maxwell: "Oh, yes. That's fine, that's fine, yes. You don't have to worry. He'll ask you all sorts of questions and give you an examination as well. They always confirm our tests by the examination. Okay?"

Litchfield: "Can it be done after 22 weeks?"

Maxwell: "I don't know. I suppose it's been done. It's pretty awful."

Kentish: "You're married as well, I take it?"

Maxwell: "Yes."

Kentish: "Have you ever had an abortion? Do you know what it is like?"

Maxwell: "I had an abortion a long time ago when I was about 18. It wasn't here. It was in Australia. They used a similar method, a suction evacuation with a local anaesthetic and not a general anaesthetic."

Kentish: "So you weren't unconscious."

Maxwell: "No."

Kentish: "Did it hurt?"

Maxwell: "No, it didn't actually, funnily enough. It was really uncomfortable, but it didn't hurt at all. No, not in the least.

"No, you won't know anything about it." More laughs. "What will happen is after the operation you just bleed for a few days. You know, just like a normal period. In fact, a lot of people have their operation at the weekend, like a

Saturday, and they stay overnight and return to work on the Monday. No, that's fine. Would you prefer to have it done on Saturday?"

Kentish: "It really doesn't matter. We haven't got anything on this Saturday have we?"

Litchfield: "I'm not sure, but after the weekend would be better."

Anyone would have thought we were arranging a bridge evening. This low-key, matter-of-fact, dispassionate and clinical dialogue was fixing the time, place and executioner for the obliteration of an unborn baby's life.

Maxwell: "Shall we say after the weekend, then?"

Kentish: "I think, actually, we arranged to see some friends this weekend."

Maxwell: "All right. What about Tuesday?"

Litchfield: "Yes, that would be a good day."

Kentish: "I was thinking about Monday, so that I wouldn't have to do the washing. I could avoid that."

Maxwell, laughing raucously: "That would be good. The chances are it would have to be Tuesday, anyway."

At this juncture, Sue Kentish left the room and changed "tapes" in the lavatory. While Sue Kentish was out of the room, Mrs. Maxwell said that abortion was a good form of contraception for girls who were not suited to the Pill. Such a remark was so outrageous and irresponsible that it was essential for us to make her repeat it on "tape" — and she duly obliged after Kentish returned.

Litchfield: "Mrs Maxwell was just saying that if you don't fancy going back on the Pill, there's no reason why you shouldn't just have another abortion."

Maxwell: "Were you worried that you mightn't be able to conceive, if you had an abortion?"

Litchfield: "Yes, she was. We also feared it was bad to have more than one."

Maxwell: "Oh, no, no." Again, this is totally at odds with current medical opinion. This was an agency advertising itself as a pregnancy advisory service and expounding dogma that the medical profession is agreed could cause permanent mental or physical damage should such erroneous advice be followed.

Kentish: "It's nice to know you've always got a get-out again, isn't it?"

Maxwell: "Yes. Yes, it is actually. And everything here is highly confidential. So nobody would ever get to know."

Strange, isn't it, that people are ashamed of having had an abortion, although it has been legalised? People do not feel remorse and guilt because they have driven *within the speed limit*. In other spheres, people do not say: "I've been good today and have abided by the law, but please, please don't let anyone find out." Is it not likely that, whatever the law, the conscience of woman tells her that abortion is fundamentally wrong? The same conscience that wakes her in the dead of night in a feverish sweat, the conscience that knots her throat at the sound of a baby's cry and the conscience that makes the aspirin bottle a more inviting proposition every time the anniversary of the abortion comes round?

Litchfield: "Should we go to the clinic today at all?"

Maxwell: "Oh, no, no. You don't have to worry about that. Just go on the day. What you do is give us a ring tomorrow morning and we'll give you the date and confirm the time as well. We'll see you again when you come back for your check-up after you come out."

Kentish: "So it's pretty certain they will do it?"

Maxwell: "Oh, yes. I think they will sign it. I would imagine so. As I said, I couldn't say to you definitely it will be fine, but, you know, I'm sure it will be all right. They do turn people away, but for extreme reasons. But I wouldn't worry too much."

Kentish: "A nod's as good as a wink?"

Maxwell: "Yes. Your first check-up will be after six weeks. You would have to have that after an operation, anyway. After that, it will be every six months."

Kentish: "How much do we owe you, then?"

Maxwell: "Um... for the pregnancy test just £1." A £1 note was handed to Mrs. Maxwell, who then asked: "Have you any more questions?"

Kentish: "Do you know who will be doing the operation?"

Maxwell: "I wouldn't know exactly which doctor it will

be, but it will be one of the gynaecologists round there. They're not general practitioners, they're qualified."

Then, we left.

A Chauffeur for a Condemned Baby

The private abortion world, like that of drugs and other underground movements, has developed its own sub-culture. The people who work in this world wear a common uniform — they talk in the same clichés, expound identical philosophies, perpetuate the same lies, manipulate the same fiddles and corruption, treat pregnant girls as pawns in some grotesque human chess game, generally dislike children and often have genocidal tendencies. When entering this world, one is instantly engulfed by its unsavoury odour and mental and intellectual uncleanliness. The whole trade smacks of the abattoir. Everyone seems bathed in the blood.

The abortion agencies are the start of the death queue. This is where the conveyor belt begins its swift and irrevocable journey to the furnace. They are very conscious of their role. If they let a pregnant girl get out of their grasp, it is less money in the bank for them and less money in the bank for the "butchers" in the clinics. Suffice it to say that very few women do get away. The programming and high-pressure salesmanship, almost tantamount to bullying, is too sophisticated and watertight for more than a few "flies" to escape the net. The girls are treated like "flies" — as small and as insignificant and as dispensable as that.

No other section of medicine has attracted such a motley crew of pirates. In fact, no other profession, business or trade — not even land and property speculation — has such a high density of "sharks". You do not find stethoscope spivs press-ganging patients into undergoing heart surgery. No one has heard of tonsillitis touts brainwashing people into undergoing a tonsillectomy. Abortion is the "black sheep" of medicine. Many of the doctors working within this twilight world could not find jobs elsewhere. Putting it bluntly, they are the "dead beats" of their profession. Most of them are bereft of ambition. They are left with the empty philosophy of the "fast buck". There are surgeons working within the abortion trade who have been either struck off or suspended from the Medical Register at some time during their career, and are labelled "undesirables" in legitimate medical environments. Quite a few abortionists have fanatical political beliefs, ranging from the disciples of Hitler to those who just wanted to reduce the world to a handful of the elite, believing as fervently in euthanasia as in abortion.

The abortion trade has even produced its own brand of specialists. The World Wide Medical Advice Service, situated in Manchester Street, London, deals mostly in fixing abortions for foreign girls, especially Germans. Abortion is illegal in Germany and a woman can be prosecuted when she returns to her country, even if the abortion was performed on another continent.

Our initial contact with this agency was made by telephone. A man answered for them and the conversation was pretty shabby. Here is how it went:

Litchfield: "I wonder whether you can help me? My girl-friend is pretty sure she's pregnant and, you know, we're in a spot of bother. We want to try to get things worked out. I said I would ring on her behalf and see what could be done." Sue was tape-recording the conversation from an extension.

Man: "Well, the best thing is to bring her along to see us, I think."

Litchfield: "Would it be best for both of us to come?"

Man: "Yeh, you can come with her, certainly, yeh. Where you ringing from now?"

Litchfield: "I'm out at Dagenham. I come into town most days and there'll be no problem coming in with her if you think it a good idea."

Man: "Yeh, you come in with her, yes. No problem. And then... um... we can arrange, you know, we'll tell you... actually the person who will deal with it isn't here at the moment."

Litchfield: "I don't know whether it makes any difference at what stage the pregnancy is?"

Man: "Well, if it's up to three months, no problem."

Litchfield: "What about if it's more advanced?"

Man: "It's still no problem. The only thing is that after three months it becomes a little bit more expensive. That's the only thing."

Litchfield: "Well, it's all right from the cash point of view. It's just a question of whether it can be done."

Man: "The thing is not to leave it too long before you come in."

Litchfield: "Is there a time limit?"

Man: "Well, four, four-and-a-half months. You know, but the thing is to have her come in. Has she had a pregnancy test?"

Litchfield: "No, I don't think so. She kept it to herself for a bit and then, finally, she gave me the old bombshell."

Man, laughing: "Yeh, the normal thing. You can come with her or she can come alone, it's the same thing."

Litchfield: "Well, if you're going to talk money..."

Man: "You'd better come with her, I should think. If she's not quite sure how pregnant she is, the sooner you come the better, for your sake, you know what I mean." Then, as an afterthought, he added: "And for her sake as well. It'll be cheaper for you. It's not difficult when she is at the later stages, but... um... you know, it depends how far pregnant she is... Let's make it tomorrow."

Sue went alone to World Wide. She used her real name and address on this occasion. The door was opened by a Mrs. Troy, a very formidable foreign woman with devil-horned-shaped glasses and a distinct guttural accent. Mrs. Troy was a big, bulky woman and she did not hesitate to throw her weight about, either.

Sue was shown into a waiting room, where a tall, sun-tanned blonde was sitting with a suitcase by her feet. "You can talk to me now," said Mrs. Troy. "This lady doesn't speak English, so it doesn't matter. Okay?"

Sue: "My boyfriend 'phoned the other day and he was told it would be all right for me to come along."

Mrs. Troy: "Are you Miss Kelly?"

Sue: "No."

Mrs. Troy: "You're not, no. Is it for a pregnancy test?"

Sue: "That's right, yes."

Mrs. Troy: "Have you brought the sample? Okay, just take a seat dear, please, would you." She took the sample into another room and returned with a form. Mrs. Troy then started to take down brief details — name, address, job...

Then, with scarcely a preamble, not knowing the circumstances, nor, indeed, whether Sue's urine was to be declared positive, Mrs. Troy said brusquely: "Now, do you want this baby?"

Sue replied: "No."

Mrs. Troy: "You don't. Now, I'm sending this sample up to the laboratory and if you are pregnant, and you want to do something about it, we can help you. But the thing is that we have to work fairly quickly. First of all, the cost is going to rise immediately after three months. They are not keen to do it after then. You haven't got a lot of time to play with. Have you any children? You haven't, no?"

Sue: "Talking about the cost, how much is it likely to be?"

Mrs. Troy: "Well, it will cost you about £140. And it's all private, then you see. It's not in a hospital. It's in a private clinic. You will have to stay in overnight. I mean, say, for supposition, you come on a Monday, right, to see me, you will be examined on that day and have some blood taken — the blood group has to be determined — then you are examined and you would go in on the Tuesday morning. You stay there all day, all night, and you come out Wednesday morning."

Sue: "And the operation would be done Tuesday morning?"

Mrs. Troy: "Tuesday morning, yes. Unless, if you particularly want it done, I mean, to suit yourself regarding if you're working or something like that. If you particularly want it to be done the weekend, this can be arranged as well."

Sue: "You'd want the money in advance, of course?"

Mrs. Troy laughed vigorously: "Well, it's not that *we*

want it dear. The doctors will not do the operating without, without the cost, you see. We've got nothing to do with it at all. It gets referred to the gynaecologist. They're all Harley Street gynaecologists."

Sue: "So it would be done in London?"

Mrs. Troy: "Oh, yes. They're all good clinics, dear. And the most important thing is the gynaecologist, which is the main thing. Any time you want children — I mean — there's no problem. You can have children. That is why we deal only with the best gynaecologists. You think you'll be able to afford this?"

Sue: "Oh, yes, I won't be paying for it. It'll be my boyfriend who is paying."

Mrs. Troy: "Mmm... so he should, shouldn't he? Now look, dear, for the result, can I phone you or will you ring me?"

Sue: "I'll ring you, if it's today?"

Mrs. Troy: "It'll be today, yes, sometime. It's got to go down to the laboratory. A whole batch went this morning, already. So I'm just trying to think of the time. Er... it's one o'clock now. If he shoots down quickly, he might do it now. Phone me about four. You've got the number? I'll give you a card. Once you go over three months, it goes up considerably in price."

Sue: "Is there any problem getting it done?"

Mrs. Troy: "No problem at all. I mean, under the National Health you wouldn't stand an earthly chance."

Sue: "Wouldn't I? Why not?"

Mrs. Troy: *"Well, what reason have you got? Tell me what good reason have you got to say that you don't want this child?"*

Sue: "None, really."

Mrs. Troy: *"Well, this is your answer, dear.* There's people waiting for months to have it done and when the time comes round, they say: 'You're too big, you can't have it done.' And you must have a reason, almost an incurable disease, or eight, nine children. Unfortunately, that is it. But it'll get better in time. Of course, the treatment in a private clinic is completely different. Completely... I mean, there's only about two or three people to a room, and you have a telephone and you're waited on. It's a rest as well."

Mrs. Troy smiled, obviously well satisfied with the working of her own propaganda machinery.

Sue: "It sounds like a hotel."

Mrs. Troy: "Well, something like. But this is why you're paying this, you see."

Sue: "I don't have to sign any forms?"

Mrs. Troy: "Nothing at all. When you come, we take all your particulars and everything, you see. But, anyway, we won't cross our bridges until we get to them. Now, £2 for the test, please."

Sue: "If I am pregnant, may I see a doctor today?"

Mrs. Troy: "Um... if you want to see a doctor today, then the operation will have to be done tomorrow morning. It would mean you would have to get the money today."

Sue: "I see, so you see the doctor the day before, then? And you also want the money a day in advance?"

Mrs. Troy; "Yes, the day before."

Sue then handed Mrs. Troy a £5 note. Mrs. Troy excused herself and returned with Sue's £3 change.

Mrs. Troy: "There's your £3 change and this is the card with the 'phone number on it."

Sue: "Will I have to go to Harley Street to see..."

Mrs. Troy: "You don't have to do anything. Now the thing is, it would be advisable, say you're having it done on Tuesday, for you to come to London, and I'd book you into a small guest house. Just for overnight, because it's rather a long way."

Sue: "Do I get examined here?"

Mrs. Troy: "No, no. You get examined... well, we've got a dozen doctors, you see, some in Harley Street, some in Welbeck Street. But you don't have to go. My chauffeur will take you and wait until you're examined. Then the following morning, my chauffeur will take you to the clinic. This is all inclusive, the fare and everything. This is how we do it. You see, we have a lot of foreign girls come over, and when you are in a country and you cannot speak the language, it is very difficult. This is the service we are giving them, you see."

Sue: "What kind of car will I be chauffeur-driven in?"

Mrs. Troy: "Well, it won't be a Rolls, that I can tell you. It'll be a car that goes, anyway. And when you are finished, the driver will collect you from the clinic and take you back to the station. It'll be perfectly all right, anyway. It's nothing serious."

Sue: "So you can fit me up at a guest house?"

Mrs. Troy: "Yes, I think it would be better, because it's a bit of a rush. You come with an overnight bag in the afternoon at about two-ish and I'll have you booked into a guest house. You go to the doctor and he'll examine you. Then we take you to the guest house. The following morning, we drive you to the clinic from the guest house. The next day, we pick you up at the clinic and drop you somewhere near where you can get a train home. Well, of course, the morning you're having the operation, dear, no breakfast, because it's done under full anaesthetic. You don't feel anything at all. You can have a cup of tea or coffee and that's all, owing to the anaesthetic, which might make you feel sick. And that's all."

Sue: "Is it a long operation?"

Mrs. Troy: "No, it's nothing. When we say operation, it's a scrape. You've never had it done before? They just clean out your womb, you see. *Which is for every woman, regardless whether or not you're pregnant, is good for them.* They clean it all out and it doesn't take very long. They're really very, very strict about things now. It's not like it was. It's extremely strict. They won't let you go home the same night, even if you wanted to. That is for your own benefit, isn't it?"

Sue: "What's one night?"

Mrs. Troy: "That's what I say. If you go and pay that type of money and you're out after four hours, it's not good for you. Now you 'phone me. My name's Mrs. Troy."

Sue departed and later that day she telephoned Mrs. Troy for the result of the pregnancy test. It is worth stressing again that Sue was known *not to be pregnant*, satisfactorily proven by one of the most eminent gynaecologists in the land. The telephone conversation, again tape-recorded, went thus:—

Sue: "Mrs. Troy? Hello, it's Susan Kentish here."

Mrs. Troy: "Yes. It's positive, dear. You weren't surprised, were you?"

Sue: "No. I've had a word with my boyfriend and he said he could get the £140, so could we go ahead and arrange something."

Mrs. Troy: "Yes, certainly. When do you want it done?"

Sue: "How about me coming in Monday and having it done Tuesday?"

Mrs. Troy: "Yes, that is fine. Are you going to stay in London overnight?"

Sue: "I thought that that would be best."

Mrs. Troy: "Well, I think so. It saves a lot of bother and rushing, you know. Can you come round about nine-thirty? I might be able to get it done for you the same day. Then you would be out on Tuesday."

Sue: "Yes, I could."

Mrs. Troy: "I'm going to try to do that, because it does save the overnight business. So be in this office not later than nine-thirty."

Sue: "Right, and which clinic shall I be going into?"

Mrs. Troy: "Well, the thing is, we have six different clinics and at the moment I can't tell you which one, owing to the question of the beds situation, you see? But as soon as you know, you can give your boyfriend a ring and tell him. After coming here, you go to the doctor and then straight into the clinic. Before you go in, you might make a 'phone call to your boyfriend from here and let him know where you are going."

Sue: "I'll only be examined once, will I?"

Mrs. Troy: "Oh, that's all, yes. Just bring a small suitcase with you, containing a nightdress. And don't have a heavy breakfast, dear, just a cup of tea and a slice of toast. No eggs and bacon, or anything like that. If you can't make it, please ring me because I'm booking this bed for you."

The appointment, of course, was not kept. The significance of this episode was the fact that everything was arranged long before Sue had even seen a doctor. Nothing whatsoever was known about her, including medical, social and economic backgrounds, and yet a bed had been booked

31

in a clinic, the financial terms had been discussed and agreed upon, and the operation was scheduled for the same day as the first and only meeting with the doctor, yet the law requires two doctors, acting in "good faith", to decide.

Abortion — "It's Dead Easy"

Kenneth Silver looks like everyone's idea of a tout. He is in his mid-thirties, he dresses "flash", displays gigantic rings on his sweaty, puffy fingers and the superfluous flesh gasping for fresh air between the buttons of his flowery shirt is testimony of the "good business, my boy" he is doing.

Mr. Silver runs his touting service, called Clinicare, from a confined room at the back of a chemist's shop at 319, Mare Street, Hackney, in the notorious East End of London. When we paid a visit to Mr. Silver, he had been advertising an "information service" every day in the personal columns of evening newspapers.

Think of all those slick, door-to-door salesmen who have irritated you or have insulted your intelligence over the past year, and you have an image of Silver. He bounced, he enthused, he boasted and he sold himself and his work as if his next meal depended upon it. No one emerged more as a "Mr. Fixit" in the sordid abortion trade than did the oily Mr. Silver. He was jolly, he was jokey, he was pushy and he epitomised everything one associates with sleazy, dubious and highly-suspect trading operations.

Bubbling with excitement and the prospect of more easy cash in his sweaty paws, he told Sue: "Your urine is definitely positive, that's for sure. No doubt about that. We do hundreds of tests a week. We're doing 500 tests a week."

We were all squeezed into Mr. Silver's suffocating little box-room, where he perched himself on the edge of an untidy desk. He had removed his jacket and his shirt sleeves were rolled up. The top button of his shirt was undone, and the knot of his spivey tie hung like a noose about his chest. He sensed trade, he smelt money and he became brisk as he engineered us towards Harley Street and his contacts who would end the life of Sue's "baby", if we could meet the price.

We have to place the word baby within quotes, just to re-emphasise that Sue was *not* pregnant, nor had she ever been.

All the time the words and their tone were being clearly and eternally recorded on our tape-recorder.

"You're round about, roughly-speaking, 12 weeks pregnant," Mr. Silver said confidently. "It depends on when you actually fell pregnant. All we can do at this stage is give you a letter to a doctor privately. If he feels that he can do a termination for you... it just depends after examining you whether he wants to do it for you.

"That's privately. It just depends entirely on the doctors. It's really a question of time more than anything else. Up to 12 weeks, it's dead easy. No problems at all. It's just a matter of whether you are 12 or 14 weeks."

Litchfield: "Well, can you fix it for us?"

Silver: "I'll tell you what we have to do. We have to register you with us. That will cost £2.50. Your number will be 444. I fill in this form..."

Mr. Silver entered our names into what he called an abortion register, which is completely illegal. This took only a few seconds, then he asked: "When do you actually want to see the doctor? Today? Are you free this afternoon?" We said that it depended where the appointment would be, in which part of London.

Silver: "It'll be in the West End of London. Okay? I fill in this form and the doctor will give you an appointment. The earliest time will be, say, a quarter to four today. And he'll just take it from there. He'll examine and if he can't do it, then we'll refund you the £2.50, because that only goes through if you are terminated."

This is absolute criminal bunkum. Abortion registers are against the law and this, in fact, was the only one we encountered throughout our entire investigation. We questioned him further on this matter and he attempted to bumble his way through.

Litchfield: "And that £2.50 pays for the registration?"

Silver: "That's for the registration, yes. They call it a

referral fee and registration. Um... that's about it, really. I don't know how much the doctor is going to charge. It really depends on him and which clinic you will be going to."

Litchfield: "Is there going to be any problem about reasons?"

Silver: "Well, no. If you're paying for the termination, they'll sort it out for you."

Sue: "Any idea how much it will cost?"

Silver: "It's impossible for me to say. Well, the maximum they'll charge you is £150. That is the maximum any doctor will charge."

Litchfield: "I thought, perhaps, it would be better to get it clear what we ought to say, or will the doctor sort that out for us?"

Here it was imperative for him to assert that neither he, nor his doctor confidante, would be a party to a conspiracy to break the law, if he was to stand any chance of keeping his head·above water. He sank miserably.

"Yes, he'll sort it out," he promised, with a wink. "There's no reason for you to make up any stories Not at all."

On this occasion, we were using the name Edwards. As Mr. Silver was making a note of this, he said: "Usually people use different names." He laughed: "We always get different names."

Sue said: "So people use false names?"

Silver kept his reply to one word: "Yes."

Litchfield: "Do we have to use the correct address?"

Silver: "No. Well, you *can* use your address. It just depends on the doctor. What I'm going to do is send you to Dr. Ashken, if he's in."

Mr. Silver picked up the telephone. "Let's have a look and see if he's in this afternoon," he said, consulting a little black book, which obviously contained the names and telephone numbers of abortionists and clinics on his list. "He's probably the quickest one," he went on, "and he's the best doctor that we know. He was in charge of Luton Hospital for about 15 years. So any cases that are at about 12 weeks, or around about there, we send to him."

Litchfield: "He's no problem?"

Silver: "No, no." There was a pause while he dialled Dr. Ashken's Wimpole Street telephone number. "It just depends, after the examination, how many weeks he says you actually are."

Mr. Silver broke off his conversation with us to talk to Dr. Ashken's secretary. Mr. Silver's end of the chat went thus:

"Hello, good afternoon, Mr. Silver here. I've got a young couple here in front of me. They could get to you by a quarter to four if doctor's in this afternoon. Would that be okay?... Um... S. Edwards... Yes. Okay, bye."

Mr. Silver turned to us again and said: "He's the best doctor there is. So there's no problem. Have you ever been pregnant before?" Sue said that she had not, which was true. She did not also add the truth that she was not even pregnant then and that we knew she could not be expecting a child.

Silver: "And you haven't seen your doctor at all? Right. It's a shame you left it so long. Three weeks ago and there would have been no problem at all!" He scribbled a note to Dr. Ashken for us to take, saying that the urine test was positive and that we wanted to consult him.

"The doctors we send people to are not the type who go bang, bang in you go and you don't see them again. Dr. Ashken will do the termination himself and he also books you for another examination about two or three weeks later."

We asked Mr. Silver if he wanted the registration money before we left. "Yes, just £2.50," he said. The only way he might say it can't be done is if it's 16 or 17 weeks. See, up to 12, 13, 14 weeks, it's not even an actual operation. It's just like a suction. There's no problem at all with that. When the pregnancy is beyond that, though, then it's a proper operation. When it's a proper operation, it's expensive. I could never tell you how much that will be. You see, we've got different doctors for different cases. If someone comes to me at six weeks, I could send her along to a doctor and he might charge £100, because it was an easy case. Your case... it's not a bad case, but it just depends on what Dr. Ashken says. He's not just a doctor who's there today and gone tomorrow. He's been practising for years."

The economics of Mr. Silver's business life do not require a qualified accountant to conclude that the abortion traffic has provided him with affluence beyond most people's wildest dreams. Financially, he is in the 'Pop' star class. The initial fee, for the urine test, was £2. On his own admission, he does 500 of those a week. That is an income of £1,000 a week. Then there was the £2.50 registration fee. His potential weekly wage is £2,250. That is a high price indeed for a job that is totally destructive rather than creative...

"How about making love to one of my patients?"

Directly opposite the fashionable Royal Garden Hotel, in Kensington High Street, London, which caters for the dollar-speaking tourists in the capital, is a narrow doorway, behind which a dusty staircase leads to the surgery of one of the most disreputable doctors in the world.

The doctor is Bernard (call me "Bunny") Mook-Sang, who comes from Guyana. His surgery looks out over the busy and bustling, but pleasant, Kensington High Street.

It is possible to sit in the hotel across the road and watch the steady flow of girls arriving with suitcases during the day at Dr. Mook-Sang's surgery. Most of them are foreign. Many of them are French. Without exception, they are seeking abortions. All his secretaries and telephonists speak fluent French. He has agents on the Continent in countries where abortion is illegal, who channel girls in Mook-Sang's direction.

Dr. Mook-Sang, a playboy who owns racehorses and loves a gamble on cards, especially poker, wagering anything up to £1,000 a go, is one of a number of doctors we stumbled across, who play what can only be described as, "both ends of the market". They arrange abortions for girls for a fee, but if a girl has left it too late and no gynaecologist can be found who is prepared to perform the operation, doctors like Mook-Sang will offer to sell the baby for the girl after its birth.

Legalised abortion has produced a drought of new-born babies for adoption in Britain. Unscrupulous doctors, acting as middle-men in baby auctions, have been able to command £1,000 or more on the open adoption market for each child.

Doctors like Mook-Sang have realised that, in today's climate, there is more money to be made from selling babies than from aborting them. It is a question of supply and demand. But Mook-Sang is none too fussy, as long as his turnover is maintained at high tide. This doctor's philosophies, preachings and way of life are destined to disturb even the most liberal and free-spirited members of society.

We met Dr. Mook-Sang in his surgery ostensibly to discuss the possibility of buying a baby through him. His role in the abortion traffic was soon apparent. In no way could he be described as shy or reticent. On the contrary, he was frighteningly forthcoming. His views, suggestions and propositions were all tape-recorded. It is right that Dr. Mook-Sang should motivate the emotion of fear, because it is his aim to up-turn and totally re-weave the fabric of British society. He talks emotionally and with passion of "Hitler's progressive thinking". He talks of the "new morality", which is really simply making society stand on its head, calling the moral immoral and the immoral moral. He sees an Alice-in-Wonderland world, everything upside down, as he peers through a perverted looking glass from his first-floor surgery window to a conventional world at which he sneers.

Dr. Mook-Sang is not alone in his morality revolution. If he were, then he could possibly be dismissed as an isolated crank, though that is not entirely feasible because he has been peddling corruption under the protective umbrella of a man of medicine. No, there is a hard coterie of abortionists in Britain — a little medical Mafia — who share Mook-Sang's extreme, fascist politics. Some are known to have people in certain Government Ministries on their pay-roll. Their aim, their pledge, is for a stranglehold. Young, frightened, desperate, pregnant girls are merely the raw material for riches.

Abortion has brought no liberation for women. It has just enabled women to be more exploited by men like Mook-Sang. Where has the money from abortion gone? — Straight into the pockets of men. Nearly all the abortionists are men. All the touts are men. Everyone who is getting rich out of abortion is a man. There must be a moral there.

Just listen to Dr. Mook-Sang. Remember, he is a

fully-qualified, registered doctor, practising in the heart of London, a man whom, by chance, you could enlist as your family general practitioner.

He leaned back in his swivel chair and placed his long hands under his chin. He was elegantly dressed and very self-assured. In many ways, a man of culture. Although in his forties, he has a babyish face, which suits his angular, lean frame. The tape-recorder purred on, immortalising every unbelievable word...

"What sort of child do you have in mind?" he said. "Are you particular about it being English? Or what about European? I've got a girl now who might come to adoption. She's nice. She's French and she's separated from her husband. She's over here seeking a termination, but she's very big and I don't think she's going to be very successful.

"I discussed this with her yesterday and I said it would be much better if she could keep the baby and arrange adoption. This is the sort of situation I'm involved in. Not very often. Say three or four times a year."

Dr. Mook-Sang said the baby would cost us £1,000. His own fee would be £200 and the mother would have a Caesarian operation. This was one of the sickest aspects of his proposition. The girl would have the Caesarian operation, even if it were not necessary, so that she would not experience the emotion of child-birth and could not possibly form any attachment to the child. It was to be a safeguard to ensure that nothing would go wrong with the financial transaction.

"A surgeon friend of mine in a nursing home told me to talk her into going to him and he would deliver her free of charge, because there are so many people waiting to adopt," he elaborated.

"This is where the law comes in again. Looking after the girl financially is where we have to be very careful, so that we don't seem to be bribing a girl to have a child. So it doesn't look as if we are saying: 'Look, okay, here is £1,000 if you have a baby.' It can be done, but then it is a bit tricky.

"Oh, we can get round that problem by paying the medical bills and looking after her for the last three months of the pregnancy, and no one can object to that.

"The important thing is convincing someone to go to term. The girl in this case should go to term and have the baby because in the end she will feel less guilty. But in her present situation it is difficult to convince her.

"She worries about the social disgrace, the society, the family. There are pressures on both sides. Unless we present her with a *fait accompli* and say, 'Look, nothing can be done,' she may run away with hysteria and just disappear. And then you lose her."

We then asked what his charges would be?

"It won't be exorbitant," he said. "You can settle that separately. Let's put it this way, it's not going to cost you the earth for my fees.

"How good is your lawyer? Get a smart lawyer. Tell him what you want to do and hear his opinion. There are no legal problems.

"Let's be men of the world. There are always ways and means if you want to jump the queue."

When pressed further regarding his "cut", he said that that was always negotiable, but, if we took the French girl's baby, his fee would be £200. It was at this point that he made what must be one of the most unethical and staggering propositions to come from the lips of a British doctor. He suggested that Litchfield should have sexual intercourse with one of his female patients until she became pregnant. That patient would carry the child, which we could adopt nine months later.

Dr. Mook-Sang gladly offered to make all arrangements, including the venue for intercourse. He said he would have to consider whether it would be preferable for the love-making to take place in his surgery or in a hotel. The patient would have to be substantially bribed, he stressed. At first, he considered the inducement would have to be in the £2,000—£3,000 region. Later he stepped up that assessment to £5,000 or £6,000. "If that is too much, I can always bribe a destitute girl to do the same for less," he suggested.

"This is literally bribing a girl to be a factory. This is terrible if you think of it in financial terms. I don't know exactly how much a bribe would have to be for. I'm just testing your flexibility.

"You don't actually have to have physical sex. You can have artificial insemination where you donate sperm and the girl is like a factory. She is doing it for money. Let's be practical.

"I don't think you would get away with less than £1,000. I am thinking in terms of call-girls. A call-girl would consider doing this for a fee. You can get an attractive call-girl. Physically, she could be vetted.

"I can find the girl. You can become the donor of the sperm and we can get her artificially inseminated. Artificial insemination as opposed to actual sex would remove all the social and emotional problems. It would be more expensive, though, because you have to get a specialist to do the insemination.

"I have a couple of call-girls who are patients of mine. They come to consult me medically. I can discuss this with them. We are good friends.

"They would only be out of operation for the last five or six months. Now, would you be interested in this French girl's baby? She is six months, but I have still to convince her to have it adopted, and if I can do this, then I can let you have a child.

"If she agrees, I'll tell her to go back to her parents and then to come back to me towards the end of January at the end of her term. I'll arrange to have a Caesarian section done and adoption can be arranged. You tell me what fees you want to stand, travel, etc., and I'll discuss it with her. This is entirely up to you. If you want to spend £200, then...

"The norm for payments would be medical fees, which, in any Caesarian section, is £500. There are surgeons' fees, there's theatre, the clinic, that's standard. The rest is what you want to give her for living costs. Paying for her travelling costs is minor, peanuts in comparison. Let's say you put a limit on what you want to spend – £800, something like that.

"You don't have to be vetted by the local authority if you are adopting privately. It's a question of discussing the legalities with your solicitor, so that he draws up the papers. Your lawyer must make sure the legal documents are done so that the girl won't go back on her decision.

"It's better for the girl not to see you. You see, from her point of view, she doesn't know anything. She doesn't have the experience of a child. All she knows is that she is pregnant and then goes into a clinic and that is that. She's out. She's relieved of a child. She wouldn't see the child and she wouldn't know who the couple were.

"We get them into the best clinics. I arrange that for you. They are privately-run clinics, beautiful. The top Harley Street surgeons perform the operations. The medical side is absolutely A1. There's no problem there. The big problem is convincing the girls to go through with this because they have got to carry it for another three months, four months, rather than having an abortion."

Dr. Mook-Sang then proudly produced photographs of himself talking to the Queen and other members of the Royal Family at a racecourse during a Caribbean tour. "I am a great racing man," he told us. "I used to be president of a turf club in Guyana. I play cards, poker, I'm a great gambler. I've staked as much as £1,000."

Returning to the subject of adoption, he said: "In adoption, a one-child family is very bad. You are going to worry too much about it if anything happens to it. You wouldn't want it to play. You would be too protective, in case it got knocked down or had an accident. You would be terrified all your life with one child."

Dr. Mook-Sang was not satisfied with auctioning us one child. Obviously, he saw the prospect of even more business, possibly an annual sale! He started to outline a plan for a kind of bought-and-bartered-for family — surely the most bizarre family planning project ever conceived.

"Once you get on with this, you ought to think of another adoption a year from now," he enthused. "You ought to think of *at least* two. Your second baby we could put into operation now by finding a suitable girl to carry Mr. Litchfield's child. That is going to take time, finding the right person willing to carry the baby for nine months. It can be done. It's an idea worth exploring because I think it is better than straight adoption.

"It's not easy to get all the conditions right. I suppose physical appearance is important. I would select a girl who looked like the wife — similar build and colouring, so the resulting baby is as natural as possible.

"You've got to make sure the girl doesn't turn awkward. You have to think of the girl's mental make-up. Obviously you want an intelligent girl. You don't want a child that is dim. It's selective mating. It was something Hitler tried to do.

"If I can get a girl, can I offer her £3,000, £2,000, £1,000... or what? It depends entirely on the girl and her concepts as to how much it would take to induce her.

"What arrangements are you willing to make? We don't want it going stroppy in the middle. How are we going to work out the business arrangements? Let's say you are detailing me to do this as your agent. What are you prepared to put down as an agent's fee to start negotiations?

"When I've found a girl, the final decision whether or not to go ahead will be yours. The point is, I might get someone who wants £1,000 or £5,000 and it will be up to you to decide whether or not to pay. Apart from a sign of good faith, the deposit will cover all the time and energy I have to waste. I will probably have to interview hundreds of girls.

"If it is a question of straight sex, you would obviously have to get to know one another. These are the services available to you. The choice is entirely up to you. If you want to put down £1,000 and give me a year to perform, fine, I'll take this on. I'll report to you once a month, once a fortnight.

"If it is unsuccessful, we can fix a few (pounds) for my time spent. If it works, you pay all the girl's expenses and inducement. It's full of legal loopholes and legal traps which a good lawyer must work out.

"If we are going to get a respectable office girl in London, she is going to want, say £10,000 — an awful lot more than the call-girl. Anyone will do it if the price is right.

"I think a call-girl is going to be interested in £5,000 or £6,000, but a respectable girl... you have to buy her morality as well. If you are using a woman as an incubator, does it matter whether she's a call-girl or a respectable girl?"

Dr. Mook-Sang's wheelings and dealings in the adoption market are not irrelevant to abortion. I think that we have adequately shown that they run parallel. Giving Dr. Mook-Sang's views on adoption at length also serves to put in profile the nature of so many of the men manipulating the abortion strings and purses throughout the world.

A few hundred yards from Dr. Mook-Sang's surgery and in the same road is the Kensington Pregnancy Advisory Service. It is run by Mrs. Jacqueline Joshua, an attractive woman in her early thirties, who dresses smartly and modestly. She is a friend of Dr. Mook-Sang and any girls going to her in search of an abortion are "fed" immediately to "Bunny" boy. Conversely, if you are a couple prepared to try to short-circuit the conventional adoption procedure, Mrs. Joshua will again help, sending you down the road to her gambling doctor friend.

One of the most objectionable aspects of Mrs. Joshua's activities in the abortion field is her involvement in negotiating "late terminations". She admitted that she had arranged for babies to be aborted up to almost seven months. The legal limit in Britain, at the time of writing, is 28 weeks, though no gynaecologist with any scruples or heart will do an abortion after 20 weeks. With today's advanced technology, there is every chance that a baby born well in advance of 28 weeks will live. But instead of taking the baby from the mother's womb and placing it in an incubator, the abortionist will throw the living, breathing, crying, thumb-sucking child into an incinerator. This is the mentality of the "late termination" abortionist. The heart is beating, the brain has been functioning since the second week through the central nervous system, the bones and body are fully formed, and it is hours, sometimes seconds, away from being entitled, by law, to life, when someone rips it from the womb and hurls it into the furnace. It is often, however, murder in the eyes of the law, because it is impossible to be absolutely sure about the pregnancy dates. Therefore, a woman believed to be 27 weeks pregnant could, in fact, be 29, and above the legal limit.

When asked if she could arrange an abortion for a girl who was 27 weeks pregnant "or more", Mrs. Joshua replied: "It's possible. But whether we can find a doctor who will do it at this stage... I know one doctor, a Dr. Mook-Sang... She needs a specialist and we can only help privately. If means are not a problem, I know a doctor who will be able to do it at this stage. We have had them done up to 26 and 27 weeks. I certainly know of a doctor who does it at the late stages."

Enough, enough, Mrs. Joshua...

Money Talk behind Lace Curtains

One of the oldest established pregnancy testing and "advisory" service units in Britain is Ladycare, owned by Mr. Thomas Pond. He operates his private enterprise from behind net curtains at 46, St. Augustine's Avenue, Ealing, London — halfway between the West End and Heathrow Airport.

Mr. Pond's headquarters is a modest private house in a modest residential area of the sprawling, shabby western extremities of the capital. The road is an avenue by name but not in character. There are trees, the occasional smell of fresh paint, a few neatly-trimmed hedges, but nevertheless, the predominant impression is one of drabness.

We arrived on Mr. Pond's doorstep one morning without an appointment. Mr. Pond, who is slim with a lugubrious face and sharp features, is in his forties. He answered the door himself, wearing a hip-length, intern-styled white jacket. It gave him the air of a medical man, although he is not one. It was with a disdaining, patronising expression that he looked down on us from his well-scrubbed doorstep.

We told Mr. Pond that we wanted a pregnancy test doing and he showed us into a waiting-room, where he took down a few brief details. We were posing as an unmarried couple again in this case. Finally, Mr. Pond said to Sue: "Would you like to come in the other room?"

Sue asked: "Can my boyfriend come with me?"

Mr. Pond replied in a surly tone: "No. I want to talk to you on your own." Sue and Mr. Pond went together into his office at the rear of the house on the ground floor. His office was small and bare, comprising a desk, chairs and a cabinet. Grubby net curtains obscured the view of the back garden. Mr. Pond asked questions relating to the possible pregnancy... "Have you been pregnant before?... Have you got the signs of pregnancy?... Do you want to wait for the result?... Can I have your £3 in advance?..."

Sue told Mr. Pond that her boyfriend had the money, so they returned to Litchfield in the waiting-room, where the £3 was handed over in cash. While doing the urine test, Mr. Pond gave us several pamphlets to read, one on abortion. This was before we had been given the result of the test and before expressing any opinions about the subject.

Mr. Pond was not away long. When he returned to the waiting-room, he declared solemnly: "It's positive. There's a report in here for you, and there's another one for you to give to the doctor you go to. It tells him what sort of test we did. And there's a copy of those notes I left you to read about pregnancy."

The great majority of the notes he had given us related to getting rid of the pregnancy rather than ways of ensuring that it thrived.

Mr. Pond expounded: "If you are going to end the pregnancy, you ought to be very quick because you are 16 weeks on from your last period. If you leave it any longer, it's going to be a complicated operation, which if done privately will cost you a lot of money."

Sue was *not* pregnant, as has been stressed many times already. Yet Mr. Pond was declaring that she was as far "gone" as 16 weeks! He also seemed to be pushing her into a fake abortion, with the phrase, "you ought to be very quick," and the warning, "if you leave it any longer... it will cost you a lot of money." Sue was not being given any time, any breathing space, time for thought. She, if it had been all real, was on the treadmill. The conveyor belt was rolling inexorably towards one of the infamous factories of death. The screw was being turned by a professional who passes on thousands of girls every year to the abortionists Also, neither of us had mentioned abortion. All we asked for was a pregnancy test. We could have been hoping upon hope that Sue was pregnant, wanting to bring a child into the world. We could have found Mr. Pond's tactless insensitive assumption that we wanted to have the baby slaughtered most offensive, even though the child turned out not to be a foetus, but a figment of the imagination.

Allowing Mr. Pond to have his head, Litchfield asked: "What can we do?"

Pond: "Have you been to your own doctor?"

Sue: "No."

Pond: "Do you want to try to get it done under the National Health?"

Sue: "I didn't want to see my own doctor."

Pond: "The only alternative is to go privately and then you pay a fee. It's £80 if it's an early pregnancy, and yours is only just an early pregnancy now. Another week and it won't be."

Litchfield: "Can it be done in that time?"

Pond: "If you go privately, yes. See a doctor today and have it done tomorrow, if you want to."

Sue: "Could we?"

Pond: "Well, if you go privately, yes."

Mr. Pond made no mention that we needed good and valid reasons under the Act. The whole tone was that it could be arranged, as long as we had the money. "Do you want to do that?" he added.

Litchfield: "Yes, and it will be eighty quid?"

Pond: "Yes, and it'll be more expensive if you leave it and more difficult to find someone to do it as well. Do you want to see a doctor today? Have you got a car here? Do you know Harley Street? It's dead easy to get to from here."

There was a respite while he browsed through a small, black contacts book. He was carrying three black notebooks containing the names and addresses of doctors and clinics.

"The doctor will be there at three," he went on. "You won't get the operation done today. You've got to see two doctors eventually. You'll see one of the two doctors and he'll make all the arrangements and tell you what to do. He may do a blood test etcetera, and the operation will be tomorrow — if you want it tomorrow?"

There were no ifs and buts, warnings or cautions, no reservation that these arrangements were dependent on our reasons for seeking an abortion being adequate and complying with the law.

"You'll be in the nursing home one night," Mr. Pond explained, getting down to specifics. "Then you'll go home the following morning. It'll be a London nursing home."

Litchfield: "What about the money?"

Pond: "Well, the sooner you can get it to the doctor, the better. Go and see Dr. Shoham this afternoon and ask him how you set about paying the fee."

Litchfield: "He'll want it in advance, I suppose?"

Pond; "Yes, they always do. They nearly always make you wait till they've cashed a cheque if that's how you're paying."

Litchfield: "Do they? Oh, well, I'd better get the cash, then?"

Pond: "Yes, if you want it done quickly. Don't worry about it, now. Ask Dr. Shoham when you get there." He then passed us a stencilled map of the part of London depicting Harley Street and Dr. Shoham's address. It also named the nearest Underground Station to Harley Street. There is no other possible way of looking at men like Mr. Pond other than as abortionists' touts and agents.

"Here you are – Dr. Shoham, 144, Harley Street," said Mr. Pond. "I don't know what the parking situation is like. You give the doctor the report of the test and keep one yourself. Go along at three. It's all right at three. He's always there Wednesdays 3–5."

Litchfield: "Reading that leaflet of yours on abortion, the only thing that crosses my mind is whether or not we qualify?"

Pond: "When you go privately, you go to a doctor who is liberal-minded. You're not going to a National Health Service doctor. And the Abortion Act says that if the doctor considers there is a risk to your mental health, he is allowed to do an abortion. The private doctors are those who consider that if you don't want a pregnancy it's going to worry you so much that there's a risk to your mental health."

This is, of course, a complete prostitution of the Act. Throughout this inquiry, we maintained that we had *no* worries, no problems, no hang-ups, and that our only reasons for wanting an abortion were entirely selfish and self-centred. In other words, we set out to buy illegal abortions. And not once were we unsuccessful.

"You read so much about the reasons you're meant to have," Litchfield commented, giving Mr. Pond the opportunity to commit himself further.

"Well, you have... yes... and he's [the doctor] got to sign a form for you, too," said Mr. Pond, as he steered us towards the door. "It's just that two doctors can have different opinions. You'll go to one doctor and he'll say, 'Well, of course you're worried about it, but there's no risk to your mental health,' and you go to another doctor and he'll say, 'Well, you can't go through with this, you're too worried about it'."

The farce is transparent. Every expectant mother is worried and concerned about her pregnancy. By that token, every pregnant woman — married or unmarried — would qualify for an abortion. Worry is an emotion. One woman can worry because she is unmarried. A married woman can worry about whether the baby will be born with an abnormality. Both women are worrying. You can argue that the mental health of both women is being impaired. The answer, though, is not to take the life of another person, another independent human being. The married woman needs reassuring that her baby will be all right. The single girl requires compassion and understanding, and people giving practical help and constructive, rather than destructive help. The unmarried mother needs admiration, never scorn. Society cannot have it both ways. If it is going to deplore abortion, it must eradicate all shame from the role of the single mother. She must be inspired to pride and not made a victim of prejudice.

. . . .

Within half a mile of Ladycare is another pregnancy testing and advisory service. This is run by a chemist from his home.

In the waiting room, there were bookshelves full of

literature on the Nazis, fascism and selective breeding and killing. There were six books entitled, "Fascism — The Only Way", three volumes were called "Hitler's Dream". Other books included: "The Importance of the Third Reich", "Mosley — The Man for Britain" and "Fascists' Forum".

"Please select a book to read," said the chemist to Litchfield while he took Sue into another room. "You'll find them all very interesting, very informative."

When they returned to the waiting-room, Litchfield commented: "There's nothing there for me. They're all about fascism and Hitler."

"Don't underestimate fascism," said the pregnancy tester intensely. "Remember, my business is all to do with selective breeding and killing. That was the great dream and immense philosophy of Hitler.

"There's a hard core of us in abortion, and that includes the doctors, who believe in the Hitler dogma. Abortion has given a great deal of power over life and death to a handful of people. We envisage a time when a mother will have the right to have a child killed up to a few hours after normal birth. When a baby is born, its mother should have a chance to look it over, ensure it comes up to specification, and decide whether or not it should live. This is the ideal, the dream, of course. We have a long way to go before this would be acceptable to society as a whole. They have to be taken along in slow stages.

"If anyone had said this at the beginning of abortion, there would have been an outcry, the public would have been horrified. You have to lead them an inch at a time. Euthanasia is next on the agenda. We are trying to compress life, to telescope and concertina it, so that life will terminate for everyone on their sixtieth birthday and the bulk of the population is aged 20–50. Most of the doctors involved in abortion whom I deal with are disciples of this cause. The doctors in Germany were ahead of Hitler — they were the ones forcing Adolf's hand for more and more experimentation. In Britain, it was the doctors who were pushing for abortion. They saw abortion as a foot in the door for more radical things. It's all to do with power and the shaping of the world."

Pin-money for the Housewives

One man who has set himself up as a pregnancy tester and abortion tout in his spare time, has housewives working for him in a little syndicate, so that his catchment area is widened.

This man is an ordinary chemist by day and an abortion tout by night. While he is attending to prescriptions by day, housewives in East London and Essex are procuring him abortion business.

Advertisements appear in local newspapers giving several telephone numbers that can be called — depending on the district in which you live — for a pregnancy test.

We telephoned one of the numbers and it was answered by a housewife who was working as an agent on a commission basis for the chemist. This is how some of the conversation went with Sue:

Woman: "5788..."

Sue: "Hello, I wonder whether you can help me. I saw your advert. this week for pregnancy testing. Can you tell me what I have to do?"

Woman: "We need the first morning's sample and we don't need a lot, only a small bottle amount. The bottle must be clean, thoroughly rinsed out, no trace of detergent. You can either bring it along or send it by post." She then gave her own private address.

Sue: "Are you a shop or something?"

Woman: "No, it's a private house."

Sue: "Have you a place nearer to me than that? I'm in Brentwood, Essex, and I see that you've got three numbers?"

Woman: "No, this would be your nearest. [Remember she is paid on commission!] One is in Dagenham and the other is the pharmacist, who does the test. He lives around the corner. But, then, he's not there during the day."

Sue: "Was that the first number I tried, the 590 one?"

Woman: "Yes."

Sue: "Whereabouts is the Dagenham one? That might be more convenient."

Woman: "I think it's St George's Road, but you'd have to ring them to arrange a convenient time, because the test has to be brought over here, anyway. I take messages for the pharmacist and also the one in Dagenham does, because, as I say, he's not there during the day. He does the tests and we have to get the samples to him in the evenings."

Sue: "So you just drop it round to him, sort of thing?"

Woman: "Yes, I should be in during the day, but if I'm out, by any chance, you could just pop it through the letter-box. It needs only to be a small bottle and we require your name on the bottle."

Sue: "And I give you the money when I get the result?"

Woman: "Well, if you could leave the money with the bottle and then 'phone that first number after six o'clock for the results."

Sue: "Oh, I see, it's not an ordinary chemist's shop?"

Woman: "The pharmacist does it from home, in the evenings."

Sue: "Do you keep any literature, if I find that I am pregnant? Or can you help me from there?"

Woman: "No, I'm afraid the pharmacist just does it all."

Sue: "I'll drop a bottle round."

Woman: "Well, if you can write your name down with the bottle so that the pharmacist will know when you call for the result."

When we telephoned the chemist at his home in the evening, the call was answered by a young girl, who called out: "Dad, it's for you..."

The girl's father came to the telephone and Sue said: "I'm ringing in response to the advert. about pregnancy testing..."

Chemist: "That's right, yes. The thing is this, you should be at least fourteen days late and, then, what we require is a specimen passed first thing in the morning. Just enough to fill a small tablet bottle. I'll give you the address... Someone is always there to take it in the mornings. If not, it's a letter-box and a small bottle will go through it. You can 'phone the same day for the result and it's £1.50."

Sue: "Can you advise me at all if I am pregnant? Can you put me in touch with a doctor, or anything?"

Chemist: "Most of them only like to handle these things at around about after the first period, or at the most, the second period, because when it gets to three months, it is quite well formed. I can give you the PAS centre. They are about the best. It's in Margaret Street. They're about the best, because they're, well, reasonably cheap. They charge only for professional services, about £60. If you go to a private clinic, particularly at a late stage, it's going to cost anything up to £200, perhaps even more."

Sue: "Money is no problem and if I can get it done privately and quickly..."

Chemist: "Well, both of them are private. These aren't the National Health, but the one in Oxford Circus is non-profit making. The other one is an ordinary clinic which runs with a profit and, of course, their charge is about £200, I'd guess.

"I don't have much to do with it. Most of the people I recommend... I'm a pharmacist, you see, so consequently, I'm not really interested in that side of it. I can send you to the PAS..."

Sue: "If they can't help me, who would you suggest?"

Chemist: "Well, there's another clinic I know. It's in Manchester Square. But, then, as I say, they're pretty expensive. It's called the World Wide Medical Service."

That is all we needed! We had come across World Wide earlier in our investigations, when they so kindly offered us a chauffeur driven car to the abortion clinic!

Sue: "You reckon that would be up to £200? That's a lot, isn't it?"

Chemist: "Yes, it is a lot. Unless you try through your own doctor on the National Health Service." (He laughed disparagingly.) "That will cost you nothing, but... er..."

Sue: "I gather it's more difficult, though?"

Chemist: "Well, you need to have a good case, you

know."

And why not? This was supposed to be the motive and intrinsic ingredients and structure of the Act.

"You'll need to have a reasonable case," the chemist continued.

Sue: "What sort of case would be best?"

Chemist: "Well, social grounds, you know, or health reasons, or things like that. Not very strong grounds, not as strong as, say, for the National Health. If you've got a reasonable case... that you don't want any more children, or you're not prepared to have children, something like that... Usually, if you give them a reasonable reason, that's good enough."

Sue: "Well, obviously, I don't want children, otherwise I wouldn't be seeking an abortion, would I?"

Chemist: "Well, no, this is it..."

Sue: "You are just a private house?"

Chemist: "That's right, yes. I'm a chemist and I do these tests at home."

By 'feeding' Sue with the reasons that would be accepted by certain scurrilous bodies for doing abortions, the chemist was guilty of inciting us to break the law.

The Only Lifeline

The advertisement in the evening paper had all the smell of the abortion tout. "Pregnant and despairing?" it asked, "then contact us for *practical* help." It had all the familiar ring of the alluring language of the abortionist's agent.

Litchfield telephoned the number given in the advertisement, purporting to be a sailor just arrived home on leave to discover his girlfriend is five months pregnant.

A woman answered the call, saying softly: "Hello, this is Lifeline."

The conversation continued:

Litchfield: "Good afternoon, I wonder whether you can help me. I'm in the Navy and I've just got back on leave and I find that my girl is pregnant. I went away about the beginning of August. I saw your advertisement in the "Evening Standard".

Woman: "She'd be five months. Do you know if she's been to see her doctor?"

Litchfield: "No, I don't think so. But she's had one of those tests. She's definitely pregnant, but she doesn't want to go to her own doctor."

Woman: "Tell me, does she live in London?"

Litchfield: "Just outside."

Woman: "Would she like to come to see us, or would she like to 'phone herself and we might get somewhere?"

Litchfield: "She's a bit shy, but I could get her to the telephone. She thought it would be a good idea if I had a word with you first."

Woman: "Well, yes, we could help her, of course. How is she situated. Is she at work or...?"

Litchfield: "She has been working, yes."

Woman: "And living at home?"

Litchfield: "She doesn't live with her parents. She lives

57

alone."

Woman: "Do you think she could 'phone us and discuss it and see what she wants to do. She really ought, of course, to go to her doctor and have ante-natal care."

Litchfield: "Would you like me to get her to the 'phone?"

Woman: "Yes, of course."

Sue then took over the conversation.

Woman: "Hello, your boyfriend has been talking to me. Did you go to your doctor?"

Sue: "No, I was waiting for my boyfriend to get back. I sent off a test and it came back positive."

Woman: "What about your doctor, what is he like? Do you feel pregnant? Are you getting bigger? So you're nearly five months' pregnant, or getting on for six. Are you working now? Where do you live? How do you feel about having this baby?"

Sue: "Well, I'm single."

Woman: "You see, the baby will be due in about three months' time. You ought to have ante-natal care. That's important and if you want to have the baby adopted, then that is quite easy. What about that?"

Sue: "Is there nothing else I can do?"

Woman: "Well, there isn't, because this baby... well, have you felt movements yet?"

Sue: "Sort of."

Woman: "You have, yes. You see it's a very big baby now."

Sue: "Couldn't I get an abortion now?"

Woman: "It wouldn't be an abortion now because it's a baby that could possibly live outside the womb. It is very much an alive baby. If you come and see us, we can get you fixed up and away from where you are, and then we can think about adoption for the baby, if you like. It's entirely up to you. Why don't you talk it over with your boyfriend and then come and see us at 39, Victoria Street, near St. James's Park Underground Station, London. What's your name by the way? Your first name will do if you don't to give it all. It's all confidential, you needn't worry. Nobody will say anything to anybody. But I think you've got to sort of settle down to it now and decide whether or not you want to keep the baby or have it adopted. If you want to get away from where you are, we can arrange for you to transfer to another doctor."

We had been wrong, thankfully. This advertisement was *not* bait dangled by the abortionists. It was the first — and only — genuine pregnancy "advisory" service we encountered throughout the entire inquiry.

Section 2: **The Doctors**

"Yes, you are pregnant!"

The entrance to 144, Harley Street, London could not have been more imposing. Wide steps, spotlessly clean and still smelling strongly of carbolic from the cleaner's scrubbing brush, led up to a massive, double-breasted door. Black-painted railings curled away at each corner of the steps and continued in both directions to neighbouring doorways.

This ancient and historic part of London has changed little in appearance over the years, though some of the men and women who work there now are remote from the past generations of medical specialists who made Harley Street a name to be revered throughout the world, in all languages, all continents, and in all dialects. It has been renowned through the ages as much for its ethics, morality and honesty as its medicine. Not any more, I'm afraid. The old brigade still stand fast, but the edges are turning yellow, like an ancient parchment, reluctantly showing signs of wear and decay. Within Harley Street, there has emerged a new and disturbing breed of men: the get-rich-quick kind who are none-too-fussy how they acquire wealth, even at the expense of *their* moral code, *their* conscience and *your* body and mind.

The solid door to No. 144 was framed in a glittering cluster of impressive brass plates. One of them bore the name of Dr. Maurice Shoham. It was to Dr. Shoham that we had been steered by Mr. Thomas Pond, of Ladycare.

. As we rang the bell, taxis were drawing up all along Harley Street. They had to pull up in the middle of the road, because every parking meter was occupied, most of them timing the stay of a Rolls-Royce, a Bentley or a Mercedes, certainly nothing "beneath" a Jaguar. At the top end of Harley Street, the traffic was already snarling up in the Marylebone Road as the afternoon-evening rush period got under way prematurely.

A woman in white who could have been a nurse or just as easily a janitor opened the door. "We've come to see Dr. Shoham," one of us said.

"Door on the right," she said curtly, and shuffled away disconsolately into the gloom beyond the stairs.

We passed by a large waiting-room. Although tastefully furnished with 'period' pieces and in no way bare, the room had a spartan atmosphere. It was a house with a split personality: there was the comfort of the past and the austerity of the present. We made our own way upstairs, and as we did so it was as if we were following a thousand footsteps, a thousand worried minds and souls praying for words of hope, comfort, reassurance, seeking a cure for mind or body. They were yesterday's people. We were part of a new traffic. We were looking for a someone who for a fee would kill an unborn baby, a baby tied and trussed inside a mother's womb and blindfolded by the placenta from which it feeds. What manner of man would we be facing? ...These were our thoughts as our feet dug into the well worn stair-carpet.

Dr. Shoham's door was wide open. He was alone, sitting behind his desk, situated in a far corner of an expansive room, which was lacking in light. The room was typical of any GP's surgery: the traditional couch, a screen, gas fire, stethoscopes, lamps, cabinets, papers and rubber stamps. Everything about it, though, was fading, bleached, threadbare and senile. One had a feeling that a million bodies and souls had been bared on that sturdy couch.

Dr. Shoham, a squat man in his fifties, with white hair and wearing black-rimmed spectacles, smiled as we entered. He rose and shook hands across his desk. We drew up chairs and he busied himself, clearing the top of his desk. His smile was friendly, disarming. In many ways, he appeared a benign, benevolent old man. There was a superficial warmth about his nature, not much depth or obvious sincerity, but he was affable.

We handed over the letter from Mr. Pond, which declared the impossible, that Sue was pregnant.

"Yes... well... actually, I don't really need any of this," he said, taking the material. "They just recommend, these agencies, where people should go. Now, I'll just get a little information from you and see how we can help you." Directing his next question at Litchfield, he said: "You are the boyfriend, I take it?"

Litchfield: "That's right. We have been living together."

Dr. Shoham: "I see, yes." Then to Sue, he said: "Have you been examined yet by a doctor?"

"No," Sue replied.

Dr. Shoham: "You haven't been examined internally, or anything like that?"

Sue: "No."

Dr. Shoham; "Well, the best thing is to check you up and see how borderline you are. I'm sure you're pregnant. It's a question of how late. You realise if it's much over 16 weeks, it can't be done as a simple procedure. It's got to be a two-stage procedure and that means you have to stay in hospital two days, instead of one."

Once again, nobody had mentioned the word "abortion", yet Dr. Shoham had assumed that all anybody could possibly want to consult him about in the world today was death to a baby. What a depressing way of earning a livelihood.

"Anyway, we'll see, we'll see," he said. "I'll soon tell by examining you and seeing exactly how big it is."

Sue: "Do you have to do an internal?"

Dr. Shoham, laughing softly: "I'm afraid so. You're very worried about that, are you? It doesn't hurt, I can assure you. Is it a question of shyness? Well, your boyfriend can sit outside. It'll only take two minutes. It is important, I'm afraid. I can't send you to a surgeon and say I don't know how pregnant you are. He'll think I'm not doing my job properly. Well, it all depends how far advanced you are, but, obviously, whatever it is, you can be helped. You realise that if it's a two-stager, it's going to be more expensive because of the nursing home charge going up?"

Litchfield: "How long before the operation?"

Dr. Shoham: "Well, if we can get her to see the surgeon today, we can get a bed for this week."

Litchfield: "How far would she have to travel?"

Dr. Shoham: "Most of the nursing homes are in London. Central London. There are one or two in outlying districts. The ones in London normally charge £100. The ones in the country or outlying areas, such as Brighton, charge £80. But it's not worth your while going down there. It would cost you more in hotel bills."

He laughed.

Litchfield: "Where could Susan go?"

Dr. Shoham: "Well, this depends on the surgeon I send you to. Most of the patients I refer go to the Avenue Clinic, Regent's Park, which is a very good one, very nice. Some go to the Welbeck Clinic, which is just off Harley Street. Basically, those are the two clinics that I use. I know they're good clinics. That's all that matters. Now, if you'd like to just take off your coat, and lie on the bed."

Litchfield: "I was a bit worried whether Sue would qualify for an abortion?"

This was the question that was guaranteed to discover whether Dr. Shoham was complying with the Act, investigating every case to ensure that the woman or girl seeking an abortion had justifiable grounds under one of the four clauses.

Dr. Shoham: "Well, as far as we're concerned in the private sector, we don't turn down any cases. We feel that if anybody wants to have a termination, they've usually made up their mind about it."

This is irrelevant. Under the terms of the Act, it is up to the *doctor*, not the woman, to decide whether or not there are sufficient grounds.

"Occasionally, you get a case of a married woman who's pregnant...she doesn't want the baby because they want to buy a television set and all that sort of thing, then I don't approve of it," he went on. "It's not worth interfering with things, then. But, by and large, certainly if you're not married, I think the wisest thing is to have something done, if you can."

Litchfield: "£100 is not too bad, is it?"

Dr. Shoham: "No, I think it's a reasonable fee. It used to be more.

"The trouble is that there is so much written about what's going on in Harley Street and a lot of it is bad. Unfortunately, girls get into the wrong hands and are asked extortionate prices. I know that £400 or £500 has been charged. But most of these villains have been virtually kicked out. There have been one or two doctors who have been absolute villains. But not only the doctors, also the people working as agents. Ladycare is all right. They're absolutely *bona fide*. They're the oldest established. They do basically pregnancies and they don't charge you anything except for the test, at least I don't think so. They just give the advice, which is fair enough. But some of these agencies take about £30 from you just to give the name of a doctor to go to. That's a shocking racket.

"Yes, well, the standard fees now are £80 to £100 for an early pregnancy throughout the private sector. We're not quite sure yet whether yours is an early one. I hope so. I don't think she looks that big."

We were not surprised considering Sue had never been pregnant in her life!

By this time, Sue had spread herself on the couch for examination. Dr. Shoham went behind the screen, felt Sue's stomach and performed a vaginal examination. It was all over in a matter of seconds. We were both fully prepared for Dr. Shoham to say that Sue was not pregnant. Despite his willingness to flout the law in other respects, it seemed inconceivable that a Harley Street doctor would set up an abortion for a girl who could not possibly be pregnant.

It is, indeed, surprising that Dr. Shoham did not notice our stunned, disbelieving faces as he pronounced: "Yes, you are pregnant. But you are not more than about ten weeks. You have probably become pregnant within the last ten weeks. So she's an early case and we can do this very quickly for you."

Talking exclusively to Sue, he said: "Now, you have to stay in hospital one night. The procedure is, you go into hospital in the morning, the nursing home, that is, and you have the operation probably in the afternoon and stay that night. In the morning, you go home."

Sue: "Are there any after-effects?"

Dr. Shoham: "No, no after-effects. Not in cases like this. I'm sorry, do you want a cigarette." He handed round a packet of Player's No. 6 tipped.

"No, no, there's no complications," he continued. "You have a period, rather like an ordinary period, immediately afterwards, and you go back to work the next day.

"There's no reason why you can't go back to work the following day. Certainly, it's advisable to take the day off, but if you have to go to work, you can."

Litchfield: "How soon can you get this done?"

Dr. Shoham: "Well, now the thing is, we have got to get you to see the gynaecologist. This is an awkward time of the day to try to contact gynaecologists and surgeons."

Sue: "Are they working in the afternoon?"

Dr. Shoham: "Yes, they're usually operating in the afternoons. Yes, unfortunately, two of them are away on holiday. Two of the people I deal with are away this week. Just this week. Coming back on Monday. Still, there's no rush. I tell you what, I'll send you round to see his secretary now and she can make all the arrangements for you for next week. Okay? It's just round the corner."

Sue: "And then it could be arranged for later next week?"

Dr. Shoham: "Oh, yes."

Litchfield: "Do we have to sign any papers?"

Dr. Shoham: "I sign the papers." He then made a telephone call. "I hope his secretary's in," he said while awaiting a reply. His call was answered.

"Hello, is Mrs. Friedman there, please? Oh, she'll be back about a quarter to five. You're sure about that? I see, I'd like to send a patient round to her. Dr. Sachs isn't back yet is he? When's he coming back, do you know? He's coming back on Monday, fine. Well, would you say I'm sending this patient round. I'm Dr. Shoham. Thank-you very much. Goodbye." He put down the receiver.

"Right, that'll save time," he told us. "She can get you organised, because they have to book the beds."

Litchfield: "Which clinic will that be?"

Dr. Shoham: "The Avenue. It's the best clinic. Now you have to see the secretary of this particular surgeon. It's in the next street, Devonshire Place. Now I've got to fill in some forms."

Dr. Shoham took out the official green abortion form. He signed it and then rubber-stamped it twice... two heavy thuds bringing the death warrant to life and a baby to death.

"This is the official Ministry form," explained Dr. Shoham. "It's all confidential. Nothing is issued. You take this with you when you see the surgeon. He has to send this off. Now, your general health is all right, is it? Are you allergic to anything like penicillin? Do you know your blood group?

"I shall put down that, on examination, the size of the uterus is that of an eight to ten weeks pregnancy." He was writing a letter to Dr. Sachs.

"Right, I'll give you my card. If you have any family planning problems... you normally get the Pill from your doctor, do you?"

Sue: "No, the Family Planning Association."

Dr. Shoham: "The FPA. I see. They're very good. They're the best. I run the Baker Street FPA. I'm in charge of that."

Litchfield: "What about the financial aspects?"

Dr. Shoham; "Well, you pay the bulk, the £100 fee to the hospital. Or the surgeon will tell you what to do the day before you go in. Um... and that's all. I have a consultation fee of £6."

Sue: "I thought we had to have two doctors to sign the form?"

Dr. Shoham: "Yes, well the doctor you're going to see on Monday, Dr. Sachs, he is the surgeon. Two doctors have to sign and one must be the surgeon. You've got to see one doctor first, that's me, before you see the surgeon.

Sue: "Will he want to do an internal examination?"

Dr. Shoham; "I'm afraid he will. He's a very nice fellow. He's a nice chap. Not only to see how big the uterus is, but also to find out its shape. After all, he's doing the actual surgical procedure and he must know what he's doing.

"Now, it's Dr. Martin Sachs, No: 8, Devonshire Place. You turn left on the main road. Better leave your car. Have you got your car parked? Well, I'd leave it. I wouldn't try to park anywhere round there. Right. That's your letter. And that's all we have to do for you."

Litchfield: "Shall I pay you now?"

Dr. Shoham: "Just as you please." Litchfield counted out six one-pound notes. "Thank you very much. Right, don't worry. You're in very good hands. You'll find it's all very straightforward."

Sue: "I'm not worried."

Dr. Shoham: "It's really quite an easy procedure. Right you are. Bye, bye."

With that, we left.

We did not go to Dr. Sach's surgery. Instead, we retained the letter and signed abortion form as documentary evidence.

The letter said: "Dear Dr. Sachs, This lady is unwillingly pregnant and on examination the size of the uterus is that of an 8–10 week pregnancy. She is in a state of neurotic depression [what humbug!] and should, in my opinion, be terminated under Clause Two. Yours truly, Dr. M. Shoham."

Have you ever heard such hypocrisy? How could any reputable doctor diagnose "neurotic depression" from Sue's comments and her attitude. We both deliberately assumed a blasé, insensitively hard approach, so that no one, in good faith, could possibly consider Sue qualified for an abortion — even if she had been pregnant, which she was not.

One of the most disturbing features is that Dr. Shoham was prepared to authorise an operation for someone whose identity he did not *really* know, and of whose medical background he was totally ignorant. Sue did use a false name. She could have died under surgery without anyone knowing the true identity of the victim. She could have had a medical history that would have made the operation highly dangerous. Yet Dr. Shoham was prepared to take her word for the fact that no such history existed. The operation would not have been recorded on her medical chart, so that any after-effects, physical or mental, could never be traced back to the abortion by her own doctor. The missing item on her medical chart could deprive doctors in the future of solving any emotional problem relating to that abortion. Traumatic experiences later in life are common among women who have undergone abortions.

Clause Two of the abortion form, chosen by Dr. Shoham, says: "The continuance of the pregnancy would involve risk of injury to the physical or mental health of the pregnant woman greater than if the pregnancy were terminated."*

The next day, we telephoned Dr. Sachs' secretary, Mrs. Friedman, and tape-recorded the following conversation:

Litchfield: "As Dr. Sachs is away, the second signature on the abortion form won't be able to be done until next week, will it?"

Mrs. Friedman: "No, no. But as you were so near to Dr. Shoham's, I thought it would be nice for you to come in and have a chat. To put Miss Wood [that is the name Sue was using on that occasion]at ease, because one is naturally a bit apprehensive at this time. Sometimes a woman's chat is better than a man's chat."

She laughed.

Litchfield: "She was a bit worried, just on the score of whether there would be any setback to the second signature?"

Mrs. Friedman: "Oh, no, no, no. Tell her absolutely nothing to worry about."

Litchfield: "Dr. Sachs isn't likely to go back on what Dr. Shoham has said?"

Mrs. Friedman: "Oh, no, no, no. He's coming back to work on Monday and that is a rather busy day, not that it really matters, we can fix her in. We can fit her in if she wants the operation on Monday. That's if you want to. It's entirely up to her. I can wait until Wednesday. It doesn't matter."

Litchfield passed over the telephone to Sue.

Mrs. Friedman: "Now Monday is rather a heavy schedule at the moment. Not that it matters. We can fix you in if you want on Monday, or on Tuesday, or on Wednesday. It doesn't matter."

Sue: "Monday would be best."

71

*See Appendix A, p.185.

Mrs. Friedman: "I'm sure I can fit you in somewhere on Monday. I'm just looking at the list to see where we can fit you in for him to see you first. Just a minute... You see we could arrange for the operation, perhaps, on Monday afternoon. So we could see you, I would suggest, about one o'clock in Devonshire Place, from where you go straight to the clinic, after he's seen you and everything."

Sue: "That would be in the Avenue Clinic?"

Mrs. Friedman: "Well, it may not be the Avenue Clinic. It may be another clinic. Were you banking on the Avenue Clinic?"

Sue: "Not particularly."

Mrs. Friedman: "Because I'll tell you the programme. If you went on Monday to the clinic, I don't think it will be the Avenue, because all the beds are taken at the moment. But it could be another clinic quite near here. It would be the London Private Clinic. If you want the Avenue Clinic, I may have to leave it until Wednesday. You don't want to wait that long? Anyway, the other clinic is also all right. It's in Langham Street. You get very good treatment and Dr. Sachs looks after you personally, sees you before and after and the next day.

"You're not to worry. That's why I wanted you to come in yesterday, so we could have a chat. I thought, as you were so near, you could have popped in and I could have explained a bit more to you. I'll explain now roughly to you what the programme will be. We'll see you round about one o'clock and Dr. Sachs will have to examine you, just to see the actual size of the pregnancy and to check on you generally. This is an important thing. You're going to have an anaesthetic and an operation after all, and no one operates on any patient without seeing her first. That would be most unethical.

"Then you would go to the clinic and have the operation. You'll be perfectly all right, but you have to stay the night in the clinic. Then the next morning, that will be Tuesday morning, you would come in here and see Dr. Sachs again, and he'll check everything is okay. He'll give you a few more instructions, what to do and what not to do. Then we'll have to see you again in a week's time for a final examination to check everything's back to normal. Your health is the main thing, therefore we take good care of you...

"The operation would be some time in the afternoon, around two-thirty or three. His programme is very full in the morning. He's operating at eleven, finishing at about twelve-thirty. Then he'll come straight back here and see you and then you go round to the clinic, which is just a few minutes from here. If this is how you want it — or if you particularly want the Avenue Clinic, you might have to wait another day. But that would be silly, really. If you come on Monday, you can have it all done on the same day."

Sue: "And Dr. Sachs fills in the rest of the form?"

Mrs. Friedman: "Oh, yes, yes. We look after you from then on, you see. Have you got the form with you? Well, bring it on Monday. What I want you to do is fast, except for one piece of toast and a cup of tea or coffee before 8 a.m., and after that, nothing at all. You have to starve before an anaesthetic.

"All you bring with you is a nightie, slippers and dressing gown, if you want to. It's not necessary. Dr. Sachs always visits the clinic after operations and sees the patients, not only after, but before the operation as well. You're his patient from then on. He looks after you."

Sue: "What about the money?"

Mrs. Friedman: "Well, you bring that with you on Monday."

Sue: "How much is it?"

Mrs. Friedman: "Didn't Dr. Shoham tell you? It's usually £100. It will have to be in cash."

Sue: "You wouldn't accept a cheque?"

Mrs. Friedman: "No, we don't accept cheques. Unfortunately, we have to pay the clinic and everything on the day, and they also like cash. They've been let down so many times with cheques and now we have to pay them cash. So, I'm afraid, it has to be cash. So I suggest you come here about one p.m. on Monday and bring your things. Is your boyfriend coming with you?"

Sue: "Yes."

Mrs. Friedman: "Oh, good. That's fine. So don't worry."

Sue: "I'm not worried." Sue kept stressing the fact that she was not worried, so that they could not say they were legitimately authorising the abortion on the grounds of mental distress.

Mrs. Friedman: "I can assure you everything is taken care of. You have anaesthetic, an injection in the arm. You don't have those horrible things over your face An injection in the arm — and you're away. And you're so well afterwards that you want to go home, but you mustn't. You've got to stay overnight. You're able to get up and walk about, and do what you like, but we prefer you to remain in the clinic overnight."

The dialogue with Mrs. Friedman is worth reproducing in full because it reveals, for the first time, the diary in the day of an abortionist, as seen from his theatre of life.

"You're really sure you know what you're doing?"

Dr. Maurice Hanley Ashken was all prepared for our arrival at his surgery at 67, Wimpole Street, London, just a few rapid heart pumps from Harley Street. He had been informed by Mr. Silver, of Clinicare, that we were on our way and had been advised of our ETA — estimated time of arrival.

Whereas Dr. Shoham had been all "bedside manner" and smarm, Dr. Ashken was more brusque, forthright, direct and terse, almost abrasive. Dr. Ashken was middle-aged, of medium height and rotund. He could best be described as looking well-nourished. He puffed at a bloated cigar and fingered his glasses continuously, as if suffering from excessive nervous energy.

The surgery was brighter and more sumptuous than Dr. Shoham's. Always near at hand was a secretary who radiated vibrations of chilly efficiency and clinical calm.

"Come and sit down, would you, please?" said Dr. Ashken. It was more an order than a request. "You've got a positive pregnancy test?"

Sue confirmed that this was correct. The test had been positive according to Mr. Silver, though Sue was *not* pregnant in reality.

Dr. Ashken virtually ignored Litchfield's existence at this stage. Talking to Sue, he asked: "Have you been to see your own doctor?"

"No, I haven't," Sue replied.

"Why not?" he demanded abruptly.

Sue: "Well, I wanted to find out for sure whether or not I was pregnant."

Dr. Ashken: "Well, you've got a positive pregnancy test."

Sue: "I went to Clinicare. Was it Mr. Silver there?"

Dr. Ashken: "Yes, I know."

Sue: "And he suggested we came to you."

Dr. Ashken: "Er... This is a laboratory test, that's all I want, to say that your test is positive. How old are you?"

Sue: "Twenty-seven."

Dr. Ashken: "Have you any children?"

Sue: "No."

Dr. Ashken: "You're the husband? Why don't you have this baby?" This was the first public recognition he had made of Litchfield's presence.

We had decided to play the role of a childless, utterly selfish, self-seeking and self-indulgent married couple who could have no possible reason in the world for qualifying for an abortion under the Act. If it was possible for us to buy an abortion with our shallow cover story, then we had proven beyond all doubt that a state of abortion on demand exists in Britain, which is contrary to both the law and the claims of successive Governments.

We assumed an attitude that should have landed us on the pavement, ejected by a disgusted gynaecologist who found us an affront to his integrity, conscience and ethics. Ejected we most certainly were not...

In answer to Dr. Ashken's question of, "Why don't you have this baby?", Sue replied: "Well, we don't want it."

Dr. Ashken: "Well, merely to say you don't want it and you're married... You *are* married?"

Sue: "Yes."

Dr. Ashken: "How long have you been married?"

Sue: "Nearly five years."

Dr. Ashken: "You really think this is the right thing to do?"

By law, it is up to him to be telling us, not the reverse!

Litchfield: "Well, we don't want a family, really."

There was silence for a few seconds.

Dr. Ashken: "You're sure you know what you're doing? You're absolutely sure you know what you're doing?"

Litchfield: "We are sure we don't want it."

Dr. Ashken: "I think before we go any further, I ought to examine you [Sue] and then we can decide. Did you decide at the time of marriage that you weren't going to have any children?"

Litchfield: "Sort of."

Dr. Ashken, to Litchfield: "How old are you?"

Litchfield: "Thirty-four."

Sue and Dr. Ashken moved into a compartment within his room, where there was an electrically-heated surgery couch. Once again Sue underwent an internal examination.

"If the couch gets too hot, tell me," said the doctor to Sue. "I thought it would be more comfortable for you like this, slightly warmed."

During the examination, Dr. Ashken asked: "Have you had any illnesses at all?" "No, none at all," said Sue.

Now comes the most revealing comment of all, the one remark that exhumes the working of the cavities of Dr. Ashken's mind at that time when, by law, he was supposed to be acting in "good faith" to ensure that only genuine cases were accepted.

"Now, the question is, what medical reason could one find for terminating the pregnancy?" he said.

"What I think I'd like you to do, is for me to ask you to go to see a psychiatrist. Go and have a word with him. If he tells me, 'yes, this is the right thing to do,' then all right "

The examination was completed and Dr. Ashken and Sue rejoined Litchfield at the desk.

Dr. Ashken immediately telephoned Dr. Phillip Maurice Bloom, a psychiatrist of 79, Harley Street. Dr. Ashken's side of the conversation went thus:

"Hello, this is Dr. Ashken here. Look, I've got a couple with me. She's 27. He's 34. They've been married five years. They have no children. There is a positive pregnancy test.

"Now, they have no children. They seem to be completely emphatic against a family and I'm just wondering whether they really quite know whether they are making the right decision. What circumstances they are taking into consideration. How they reached their view-point. And I would like you to investigate this case for me. After all, this is more, very much up your line.

"And the question of whether a therapeutic termination is to my mind something which one would have to give very

77

serious consideration to. I would like you to tell me what you think. All right? Right, Thank you. Bye-bye."

Returning to us, he said: "That's Dr. Phillip Bloom. You go there now. After you've been to him, come back and see me with his report. And we can discuss it. Pay him his fee when you see him."

Sue: "How much will that be?"

Dr. Ashken: "Round about ten. He usually charges about ten guineas, the normal consultation."

Litchfield: "How far gone is my wife?"

Dr. Ashken: "Well, I think you're about eleven to twelve weeks. Not more."

This was the second doctor in the abortion trade to internally examine the unpregnant Sue and diagnose her pregnant, though, as you no doubt have noticed, the stage of the phantom pregnancy fluctuated... and continued to do so throughout the inquiry.

We left Dr. Ashken with a note from him for Dr. Bloom.

"Were you a bed-wetter as a child?"

Dr. Phillip Maurice Bloom was a sombre, elderly man with a sorrowful, Spaniel face. He wore pin-stripe trousers, black jacket, Eton collar and a waistcoat, from which a watchchain hung in a loop. There were no highs or lows to his voice. He spoke slowly in a monotone that was almost hypnotic. He looked like a living relic from a bygone age that had transcended generations, defying the call of the grave.

Dr. Bloom's office was a tiny room, resembling a tutor's study, at the end of a long, meandering corridor on the ground floor.

The complete dialogue of this interview warrants reproduction because it illustrates the farce of it all. We were all just going through the motions, knowing, in advance, the outcome and the conclusions. It was a horrible, shameful sham.

Dr. Bloom: "When were you married?"

Sue: "It'll be six years this year."

Dr. Bloom: "You have no children?"

Sue: "No."

Dr. Bloom: "Have you ever been pregnant?"

Sue: "No."

Dr. Bloom: "I understand that you don't want this pregnancy?"

Sue: "That's right."

Dr. Bloom: "You both don't want it? You're absolutely certain of this?"

Sue: "Yes."

Litchfield: "Yes."

Dr. Bloom: "All right. Now, I'd like to see your wife for just a few minutes alone first. So if you'd go into the waiting room..."

Litchfield retired to the large waiting-room at the end of the corridor beside a porter's lodge within the building. The "interrogation" began.

Dr. Bloom: "Have you a big family?"

Sue: "No, just myself and a brother."

Dr. Bloom: "How old's your brother?"

Sue: "He's two years older than me. Well, 18 months."

Sue was giving honest answers about herself and her *real* family and background.

Dr. Bloom: "What's your family background like? Is it pretty ordinary, or what?"

Sue: "Yes, my father's a printer. My mother worked with him because they had a shop as well. I went to local schools. Failed the 11-plus."

Dr. Bloom latched on to that immediately. "You failed it?" he said. "Was that a blow to you and your family?"

Sue was determined not to give him any scope. "Not to them," she said. "They're not the sort who would worry about that."

Dr. Bloom: "Why did you fail it? You didn't work or... not because of lack of intelligence?"

Sue: "Well, I always say that I was born at eleven, that I started working as soon as I went to my secondary school. I just think that children develop at different ages."

Dr. Bloom: "Parents get on together?"

Sue: "Yes."

Dr. Bloom: "No rows?"

Sue: "No. I've never seen a happier couple actually. They're extremely lucky, I think."

Dr. Bloom: "Any nervous or mental breakdowns in your family?"

Sue: "No."

Dr. Bloom: "Mother or father never been under a psychiatrist or doctor for their nerves, or anything like that?"

Sue: "No."

Dr. Bloom was finding it hard going. Sue was giving away nothing that he could capitalise on.

Dr. Bloom: "Were you happy as a child?"

Sue: "Yes, yes."

Dr. Bloom: "Was your mother a strong personality?"

Sue: "No, my father was the dominant personality, I would say. Yes, very much more so than my mother."

Dr. Bloom: "What were you like as a child?"

Sue: "In what way?"

Dr. Bloom: "Personality?"

Sue: "Um... it's almost impossible to say. I don't remember having a particularly strong personality as a child at all. I was a happy child. Shy, I think. Self-conscious."

Dr. Bloom: "Why was that, do you think?"

Sue: "No reason I could put my finger on. I just was. Born that way, I suppose."

Dr. Bloom: "Did you get on with children, the other girls at school?"

Sue: "Yes, yes." She saw that one coming and all that it implied!

Dr. Bloom: "Made friends quite easily?"

Sue: "Yes."

Dr. Bloom: "Did you have any nervous breakdown at all? Or nervous trouble?"

Sue: "Oh, no."

Dr. Bloom: "Nothing like that at all?"

Sue: "No."

The man is becoming desperate!

Dr. Bloom: "Were you a bed-wetter as a child?" The psychiatrist's immortal solution to everything!

Sue: "Yes, I don't actually remember wetting my bed, but my parents have talked of it since. What child hasn't wet its bed? All babies do it most of the day!"

Dr. Bloom: "About what age?"

Sue: "Well, I would have stopped before I went to school, probably about four, I think."

Dr. Bloom: "You have asthma, or eczema, or skin disease, or anything like that?"

Sue: "No."

Dr. Bloom: "What conditions or illnesses did you have as a child?"

Sue: "Well, I would have had all the usual ones. Um... I had my tonsils out. I don't think I had any, apart from the ordinary — scarlet fever, I think that was about the most unusual I had."

Dr. Bloom: "Your mother and father gave out a lot of affection, did they?"

Sue: "Yes."

Dr. Bloom: "What were you like as a teenager — were you shy, self-conscious, would you say?"

Sue: "Yes, I think so, more than when I was younger; a bit of an isolationist, but by inclination."

Dr. Bloom: "A loner?"

Sue: "A bit of one, but by choice. I'm quite happy with my own company."

Dr. Bloom: "Occasional depressions sometimes?"

Sue: "Yes, like most people. You know, sometimes things get me down a bit."

Dr. Bloom: "Up and down as a teenager?"

Sue: "I would say that I was fairly even-mooded and occasionally I have off days, like anybody."

Dr. Bloom: "How old were you when you left school?"

Sue: "Sixteen."

Dr. Bloom: "You got married when you were about twenty-two?"

Sue: "Yes, that's right."

Dr. Bloom: "How's your marriage been?"

Sue: "That's been fine. It's working very well."

Dr. Bloom: "Sex side all right?"

Sue: "Yes, very good, actually."

Dr. Bloom: "Do you get satisfaction all right?"

Sue: "Yes, yes. We're quite lucky, we're happy together."

Dr. Bloom: "Have you had any upsets with people at all in the past few years?"

Sue: "No, I'm not one to have upsets, in the sense that I would avoid them."

Dr. Bloom: "You keep your emotions to yourself, do you?"

Sue: "Yes, I do. I'm not one to go crying on people's shoulders. But, obviously, I share things with Michael."

Dr. Bloom: "Do you sometimes feel very tight inside?"

Sue; "Yes, you know the normal thing, if people get you on edge, clenching muscles inside."

Dr. Bloom: "And how does it show up? Do you have tummy troubles, or anything like that?"

Sue: "No, no. I suppose the only way it shows up is that I smoke a lot."

Dr. Bloom: "How many cigarettes a day do you smoke?"

Sue: "About sixty, forty to sixty."

Dr. Bloom: "Do you do anything else like that? Do you tend to be a perfectionist in the office or the home?"

Sue: "Yes, I suppose I do try to be a perfectionist. In things I do, I like to do them well. I always feel I fall quite a bit short of that."

Dr. Bloom: "Is your mother a person like that?"

Sue: "No, my mother's not like me. I would say that I was more like my father."

Dr. Bloom: "Was your father more important to you than your mother?"

Sue: "Yes, well... more important? Yes, I suppose so, because I saw less of him. He was a more distant figure."

Dr. Bloom: "Are you the type of person who likes to have things really neat and routine on your desk?"

Sue: "Theoretically, yes, but in practice, it doesn't work out like that."

Dr. Bloom: "When did you give up your job?"

We had decided that Sue should wallow in the role of a woman of leisure, who would have all the time and amenities for bringing up a child, without it being a threat to our standard of living.

Sue: "It would be about three years ago now."

Dr. Bloom: "What do you do with yourself all the time?"

Sue: "Apart from the normal housework routine, which obviously takes a fair bit of time, I have lots of friends and I have an active social life during the day."

Dr. Bloom: "What do you do?"

Sue: "Well, it's a very lazy life. One or two mornings a week I visit friends for coffee."

Dr. Bloom: "You don't particularly want to work?"

Sue: "No, there's no need for me to work."

Dr. Bloom: "Do you like to do housework?"

Sue: "I don't actually enjoy doing housework. I enjoy the finished product, and I like to be home, obviously, when Michael gets in."

Dr. Bloom: "You never wanted to have children?"

Sue: "No."

Dr. Bloom: "Any idea why?"

Sue: "No inclination for them, really."

Dr. Bloom: "You don't swoon over babies?"

Sue: "No. I mean, I like other people's babies. Some of my friends have babies."

Dr. Bloom: "Are you afraid of the pregnancy or of bringing the baby into the world?"

Sue: "No, because I suppose the actual birth doesn't last that long, does it?"

Dr. Bloom: "Were you a bit spoiled as a child?"

Sue: "Yes, I was."

Dr. Bloom: "Protected, were you?"

Sue: "Yes, I was. I had a protected upbringing, certainly."

Dr. Bloom: "And you have no feeling at all that you want a child?"

Sue: "No."

Dr. Bloom: "Absolutely none?"

Sue: "No."

Dr. Bloom: "What about your husband?"

Sue: "No, he doesn't, either."

Dr. Bloom: "He doesn't, either. He's rather a quiet fellow, isn't he?"

Sue: "Yes, he's got a bit of tonsillitis at the moment."

Dr. Bloom: "A mild-mannered man, is he?"

Sue: "Yes, he is a mild-mannered man. He's a man of definite views."

Dr. Bloom: "Does he come from a big family?"

Sue: "No brothers or sisters."

Dr. Bloom; "He's the only child, is he?"

Sue: "Yes."

Dr. Bloom: "Did he have a normal upbringing, too?"

Sue: "Yes."

Dr. Bloom; "He was rather petted by his family, too, I suppose?"

Sue: "I think it was a pretty normal one, as far as I know. He didn't have a rough upbringing or a bad one."

Dr. Bloom: "You spoke to your own doctor about this, or have you not been to him?"

Sue: "No, I haven't been to my own doctor."

Dr. Bloom: "There's no worries?"

Sue: "No."

Dr. Bloom then telephoned the porter's lodge at the entrance of the building and Litchfield was informed that he could re-join the interview.

Dr. Bloom, before Litchfield had reached his office, said: "You don't think that you're going to be lonely later on if you don't have children?"

Sue: "No, I don't think so."

At that juncture, Litchfield re-entered the room.

Sue: "Do you think we will be lonely later on if we don't have children, Michael?"

Litchfield: "I don't think so."

Dr. Bloom: "How do you get on with your parents, all right?"

Sue: "Yes, fine."

Dr. Bloom: "Are your parents alive?"

Litchfield: "Yes, they are."

Dr. Bloom: "Get on with them all right?"

Litchfield: "Yes, fine."

Dr. Bloom: "You don't want to have children, either?"

Litchfield: "Um... well, you know, we didn't plan to have them at the moment. That's as far as I've really thought about it."

Litchfield deliberately showed ambivalence, giving Dr. Bloom the opportunity to pounce on this hesitation and amplify the magnitude of what we were contemplating.

Instead, Dr. Bloom proceeded: "Have you any yearning to have babies in the home?"

Litchfield: "Not at the moment."

Dr. Bloom: "So you might want some one day?"

Sue: "That's something for the future, isn't it?"

Dr. Bloom: "You don't feel that way at the moment?"

Sue: "No."

Dr. Bloom: *"Well, I don't see any purpose in having a*

85

child you don't want. You've thought of having it adopted, have you?"

Sue: "No, we hadn't thought of that, actually."

Dr. Bloom: "You don't want to go through with the pregnancy?"

Sue: "No."

Dr. Bloom: "You're a hundred percent certain that you want the pregnancy ended?"

Sue: "I think that would be the best thing, don't you?"

Dr. Bloom: "I'm asking you what you think?"

Sue: "I think so, yes."

Again we falter, almost begging Dr. Bloom to argue the case of the child, to fight for a life to be spared.

Dr. Bloom: "You feel a hundred percent certain that you don't want it? You want to end it?"

This approach was forcing us into a corner. It was destined to harden our opinions, rather than question them.

Sue: "Yes."

Dr. Bloom: "And do you agree?"

Litchfield: "Yes."

Dr. Bloom: "Well, yes, I don't think an unwanted child is a good thing to have. You're the type of person who would probably go through a fair amount of mental stress, and if you're inclined that way, you're probably inclined to be a worrier, too. Are you?"

Sue: "Um..."

Litchfield; "I wouldn't have said that you were a worrier."

Dr. Bloom: "Not particularly a worrier?"

Sue: "No."

Dr. Bloom: "Does she brood? Does she cling on to something when she gets her teeth into it? Sort of worries it?"

Sue: "I'm very tenacious."

Dr. Bloom: "That's what I meant. And you sometimes worry about something you might have done? Written a letter and sent it off and said, 'Now I wonder whether I shouldn't have written something else'?"

He seemed desperate to get Sue to admit that she was a worrier, but we had no intention of providing him any solace or excuse for putting his name to an abortion consent form.

"Oh, no," said Sue. "After I've done it, it's done, and that's it."

Dr. Bloom: "You never go out of a room and come back to see whether you turned off the light?"

What a joke!

Sue: "No, I think if it's on, then it's on. Or if the house burns down, it burns down."

Dr. Bloom, to Litchfield: "What sort of personality is she, would you say?"

Litchfield: "Easy going. Very easy to live with. Any particular sphere you're thinking of?"

Dr. Bloom: "No, I just wondered how you see her. How you would describe her to me, what sort of personality?"

Litchfield: "Quite serious, you know. A thinking person. She wouldn't undertake anything lightly."

Dr. Bloom: "All right now. If you'd just settle back for a moment, I'm just going to write a letter to Dr. Ashken. I'm writing this letter now, otherwise, if I dictate it to my secretary, it won't get to him so soon."

Sue: "We've got to go back to him, so shall we take it with us?"

Dr. Bloom: "Yes, that's the idea. He wants to know what's going on, what I think."

There was a long pause, after which he said: "I shall sign the form for you to take back to Dr. Ashken."

Sue: "Do we have to sign that form?"

Dr. Bloom: "No, this is just the official form that the Government wants, just making a note of what grounds are given for terminating the pregnancy. That goes into a file, never to be seen again."

Sue: "And what grounds will it be?"

Dr. Bloom; "On psychological grounds. You're not physically unable to have this baby, you're not going to be physically hurt by it. So I put that you're going to react very strongly psychologically... which is what I'm putting down. It's what the Government wants to know, or what Parliament says the Government wants to know, their duty to want to know."

Sue: "They just file it away somewhere, I suppose?"

Dr. Bloom: "This goes to Government headquarters, the Ministry of Health and Social Security. And, as I told you, when they get it, they look at it, they note that it's been signed by medical people and they look to see for what reason the abortion has been done. And they make a note of these two things and put it away. It's just a few statistics. It's routine."

Just *routine*, just another death, just a statistic, just a little fact to be lost in a fatuous file...

"Take this back to Dr. Ashken. He'll read my letter and I think he'll probably go ahead now. My secretary is off by now, so you'll have to pay my consultation fee."

Litchfield: "How much is that?"

Dr. Bloom: "Ten guineas."

Litchfield exchanged ten guineas for the signed abortion form and the letter to Dr. Ashken.

"Thank you very much," said Dr. Bloom. "Right, you go straight back to Dr. Ashken."

We did not return to Dr. Ashken. Instead, we retained the signed and stamped abortion form and also Dr. Bloom's letter, which we publish here.

The letter from Dr. Bloom to Dr. Ashken, which we have retained, said:

"This patient, the younger of two children, was somewhat spoilt and protected as a child. Her parents both worked in the business they owned and I think, possibly, there were elements of deprivation in this situation.

There are symptoms of some early disturbance. She was a bed-wetter and, in her teens, she was shy, uncertain and a loner. She withdraws in stress, but feels all tight inside.

She is also obsessional, shown up in smoking 50 cigarettes a day and being a perfectionist in anything she does. In fact, she retains a feeling of guilt in not coming up to scratch. She has no maternal feelings, is an emotionally immature person and could react very neurotically to a pregnancy forced on her.

Her husband was an only child, is a passive personality and is neurotically dominated by her. She manifests a reactive anxiety state and I think, under the circumstances, I would agree that termination is advisable."

It would seem that no comment could be more succinct or deprecating than the letter itself. One merely has to read the transcript of the interview with Dr. Bloom and then study his letter to be immediately aware of the farce. There is more to getting pregnant than having wet one's nappy as a baby!

Immediately after leaving Dr. Bloom, we telephoned Dr. Ashken. We said that the abortion form had been signed by Dr. Bloom.

Dr. Ashken said: "Oh, has he? That's fine."

We asked Dr. Ashken if he would sign also and he replied: "Yes, when you come to see me. I shall be able to do the operation this weekend, probably at a clinic in North London."

The importance of the transcript of the interview with Dr. Bloom is that it establishes beyond all doubt that there is abortion on demand in the private sector. No one could contend that Sue's answers depicted anything but a completely normal and balanced adult. If she qualified for an abortion on that interview, then *no* woman is fit to bear a child. Dr. Bloom simply kept asking whether or not we wanted the child. To say that you do not want the child and have an abortion on those grounds is abortion on demand. The doctors are supposed to establish, regardless of the wishes of the mother, whether or not it will be *harmful* for her to have a child. The distinction is not *that* subtle.

We demanded, not very energetically, almost tacitly, in fact, an abortion for Sue, and it was signed and sealed without any sweat or tears. Just a few grubby pound notes. That's all it needed...

Section 3: The Charities

The "Charitable" Way of Killing

The Brook Advisory Centre occupies four floors at 233, Tottenham Court Road, London. From the outside, it looks a drab, faceless place, as anonymous and characterless as the crowds that surge past from early morning until late at night. Inside, however, the decor was cheery and bright. There was a fresh atmosphere, without the antiseptic odour associated with medicine parlours. The walls were painted in pastel shades. All the staff wore spotlessly clean white overalls. The magazines were glossy and relatively new — by waiting room standards. Tea, coffee and biscuits could be bought while patients were waiting to be seen by the doctors.

We decided to telephone the Brook Advisory Centre first, just to get a "feel" of the place, so we knew something of its attitudes and idiosyncrasies in advance. Sue spoke to a woman in the "pregnancy department", who apologised for the length of time taken by her to answer the call.

"I'm pregnant," said Sue, not being over-generous with words. "I wonder whether you can help me?"

"Just come in with an early morning specimen of urine, please. What is your name?"

Sue used the name Susan Clarke on this occasion. "If you can help me, how quickly could I get it done?" Sue pushed.

"Well, it won't take very long," promised the woman. "If the doctor decides he can help you, it will go forward straight away, within a few days."

Sue had asked if the Centre could help her, and the woman had immediately assumed, without any prompting, that an abortion was being sought. Here again we were witnessing the abortion mentality: abortion has become so commonplace and so universally prevalent that it was beyond this woman's comprehension that Sue could be telephoning for a reason other than abortion. In a way, she is a sad reflection of the abortion syndrome. She is as much a casualty as are the babies who are slain while sheltering in their mother's womb.

Sue asked: "How much will it cost?"

"Ah! That I couldn't tell you."

Sue: "Any idea at all?"

Woman: "Well, you might be able to get it on the National Health. But that is the sort of thing you will have to discuss with the doctor. I couldn't say now."

Sue: "But if I don't get it done on the National Health?"

Woman: "Privately? I don't know." There was silence before she called to someone in the same room: 'How much will be the cost of an abortion?' She was provided with the details and she resumed her conversation with Sue. "Anything between £50 and £70," she said.

Sue: "Is it all right if I come in with my boyfriend?"

Woman: "You can bring anyone you like with you, so long as you bring your specimen. That's what will count." She laughed loudly.

Sue: "I'm not planning to bring the whole family."

Woman: "Look, darling. I've got a queue down the front of the desk. I've told you that you must bring in a specimen. Bring your boyfriend, your aunt, your ma or your uncle. What your boyfriend thinks about it is immaterial. It's what the doctor here thinks about it. Right, okay, bye."

With that, the funny lady of the Brook Advisory Centre hung up.

When we attended the Brook Advisory Centre four days later, Sue adopted her middle Christian name, Joy, and her maiden name, Wood. For this test, we played the parts of a single girl and a married man having an affair.

At the reception desk, Sue said: "I think I'm pregnant. I've brought a urine sample and I wonder whether you can help me?"

"Go upstairs and see the appointments clerk.", the receptionist instructed.

Sue climbed to the second floor, where the appointments clerk asked: "Are you registered with us?"

"No, I'm not," Sue replied.

Clerk: "Is it about birth control?"

Sue: "No, I think I'm pregnant."

Clerk: "Well, you want a test doing."

Sue: "Yes, please. I've brought a sample."

Clerk: "I see. What's your name?" Sue gave the details, and asked: "How much do you charge for the test?"

Clerk: "Nothing. It's free. How did you hear about the clinic?"

Sue: "I'm not quite sure."

Clerk: "Have you got a doctor?"

Sue: "No."

Clerk: "Here's your appointment card. You'll need that when you come again."

Sue: "Who do I have to see?"

Clerk: "You have to see the nurse." Sue was shown up another flight of stairs, to the third floor, where she was seen by a nurse. Again it was another question-and-answer session.

Nurse: "How old were you when you had your first period?"

Sue: "About twelve or thirteen."

Nurse: "Did you use any form of contraception, or did you just chance to luck?"

Sue: "My boyfriend was using the sheath."

Nurse: "Well, we always feel it's better, if you use the sheath, for the girl to use a pessary... Do you feel as if you're pregnant?"

Sue: "Yes. I don't know whether you can help me if I am?"

Nurse: "I think so."

Sue: "Only I don't know how difficult it is to qualify for an abortion?"

Nurse: "Well, see what the doctors have to say. You need more than one for that."

Sue: "More than one doctor?"

Nurse: "You'll see a doctor today and you know, there will be other talks about it. How did you get to know about

95

us?"

Sue: "I'm not quite sure. I knew the name."

Nurse: "It's in the newspapers. Lots of our people go on television." The nurse started testing the urine.

Sue: "That's fascinating, what do you have to look for?"

Nurse: "Well, I look for changes... there's a look to it..."

Sue: "Does it cost a lot for you to help me?"

Nurse: "If it's a National Health one, it doesn't cost anything. But if it's not, the ones they arrange here run at about £60. I'm a speaker for the FPA. Not here, I work for the FPA in Sussex. I come up from Guildford. It's a long journey. It does look as if you're pregnant, my dear. (Not another fake pregnancy, Sue thought to herself!) It does, I'm very sorry. Well, you felt it, didn't you? I mean, you knew yourself."

It was the one thing Sue KNEW she could not possible be.

Sue: "You lecture to FPA workers, do you?"

Nurse: "Midwives, that sort of thing. It's okay lecturing to your own people, but these young wives' meetings, they're awfully eager to know. But you have to be careful what you say, you know. You don't want to offend them in any way."

The nurse left the room for a short time and when she returned, she said: "It is positive. You want to see somebody about it? Well, our doctor is just due to go off. I'll see if I can get somebody else."

Sue: "How soon do you think I can get it done?"

Nurse: "Very soon, I should think. But we'll have to leave that to the doctors to say. Now I'll make you an appointment for 2.15 this afternoon to see a counsellor, and then you'll see Dr. Chisholm."

In the afternoon, the counsellor, who is also a magistrate, literally foisted an abortion on Sue, saying: "Trying to bring up a child as a single girl is not to be recommended. It can be done, but I don't advise it." And turning to Litchfield, she said: "And it wouldn't do your marriage much good, would it? No, an abortion seems the only answer."

This was not abortion on demand. It was tantamount to

abortion by persuasion.

Next stop was the fourth floor, where we both saw another nurse, who possessed hard, uncompromising, cruel features. Her eyes were icy and unsympathetic. Her lips were thin, mean and pursed. In her white smock, she looked as inanimate as marble. Her name was Fletcher.

"The report is all right from the counsellor, is it?" Litchfield inquired.

"Yes," said the nurse, "and you are going in to see doctor. Yes, that will be all right. You are going to see Mr. Naylor, but first it will be Dr. Chisholm, who will examine you. Dr. Chisholm has agreed to see you. He's really very nice. You can both go in together if you want to."

Sue: "And will Mr. Naylor see us this afternoon, too?"

Nurse: "Maybe tonight. He's very good, Mr. Naylor "

Litchfield: "So she'll get it all done and signed up today?"

Nurse: "I should say so. The quicker the better. You're not worried, are you?"

Sue: "No, you have to take these things philosophically, don't you?"

Nurse: "Well, of course. It's something that overtakes you and you have to decide what is best. Only you can decide, after all. You're two people and you're fully mature, and you work it out and come to a sensible decision. Without any sentimentality. You just have to weigh up everything. And be sensible about it."

Sue: "What about the people who are against it?"

Nurse: "Well, they're against it for various reasons. The world is horribly over-populated and not happy."

Now they are saying happiness is abortion-shaped!

The nurse expounded further: "You should only have children when you want them, at the time you want them, and that is it. That's what think. Not when nature decrees, because she decrees far too often, if you're fertile. I can tell you. It's the easiest thing in the world to get pregnant."

The woman is unbelievable! I assure you she is *real* and not a fictitious character introduced to add a tinge of light relief, like a court jester.

She goes on: "I've gone all my life not to. Very happily

97

married and all that. I mean, I know exactly. But... er... I have three sons and that's that. A very severe miscarriage and they said 'You'll never have any more.' and I didn't. That was all right, wasn't it? But that was an accident." She laughed hideously.

Thankfully, we were spared more of her pearls of wisdom by being summoned by Dr. Alexander Chisholm. He was an absent-minded looking middle-aged man, tall, slim and stooping, his shoulders well-rounded. He wore spectacles and he peered above them as he studied us across his desk.

Dr. Chisholm obviously had not been too well briefed. "You are Mr. and Mrs. Wood, I take it, are you?" he said by way of an opening gambit.

"No, we're not," said Litchfield.

"I'm Miss Wood," said Sue.

"And I'm the boyfriend," said Litchfield.

Dr. Chisholm: "The boyfriend (he laughed gently) yes, that's right. I haven't seen you here before. You're here for the first time, I take it?"

Sue: "That's right, yes."

Dr. Chisholm, opening the file: "And you've been talking to the counsellor... er... what was that about? I haven't had a chance to have a word with her yet."

Sue: "She was asking whether I wanted the baby or not, and all about it."

Dr. Chisholm, somewhat surprised: "Are you pregnant? Oh, I see. I didn't realise that. I haven't had time to look at the notes, yet. Yes, (looking at the file more closely) it was a positive pregnancy test. And it's not possible for you to go on with it, is it?"

Sue: "No, it wouldn't be very convenient. She (the counsellor) has made a report there."

Not convenient... we should have been tossed into the street as befits the trash and garbage we were portraying.

Dr. Chisholm: "I'll just read this. You feel it's an impossible situation at this point in your relationship?"

Sue: "Mmm..."

Litchfield: "Yes."

Dr. Chisholm: "Right, now I'll just run through the

history here. You don't want to have this happen again. It's very distressing. Not from the medical or physical point of view so much as the emotional aspect. Now what about your doctor, may I write to him? To let him know you're going on the Pill afterwards, or would you prefer me not to write?"

Sue: "I'd prefer you not to. Let me think about it."

Dr. Chisholm: "Yes, certainly, we'll leave it open. What past illnesses have you had? Have you had anything seriously wrong?"

Sue: "No, I've been very lucky. Just the normal children's ailments."

Dr. Chisholm: "You're not on any treatment at the present, are you?"

Sue: "No."

Dr. Chisholm: "And have you had any operations of any kind?"

Sue: "Yes, I had one for an ovarian cyst and my appendix..."

Dr. Chisholm: "Do you happen to know your blood group?"

Sue: "No idea."

Dr. Chisholm: "Has either your mother or your father had any high blood pressure or heart disease?"

Sue; "No."

Dr. Chisholm: "Any diabetes in the family? Have you ever had jaundice? Do you suffer from headaches or migraine? Do you ever wear contact lenses? And you've never been pregnant before?"

Sue: "No, no, no, no, no."

Dr. Chisholm: "Yes, right. Well, that all seems perfectly straightforward. I think if it's convenient today, I'll do an internal examination to determine the stage of your pregnancy. And I'll also, I think, do a smear test for you, at the same time."

Sue: "What's the point of the smear?"

Dr. Chisholm: "Well, it's simply a cancer exclusion thing, we'd do it anyway. It's nothing, don't worry, there's nothing to it. It's all part of the examination."

Sue: "Can it harm the foetus?"

Dr. Chisholm: "Oh, it won't do any harm at all. No, no, er... I take it that you've decided you do want the termination?"

Sue: "Yes."

Dr. Chisholm: "And there's no question of your...?"

Sue: "No. The smear wouldn't have any effect anyway, would it?"

Dr. Chisholm: "I would say absolutely not. But probably, if you were going on with the pregnancy, I would avoid doing these examinations, I think."

This is an important point; a girl could have the examination and then change her mind about having the abortion, but the harm could already have been done. Dr. Chisholm certainly suggested there was a risk involved for anyone "going through with a pregnancy".

Dr. Chisholm went on: "I mean, your mind is quite made up? I assumed, rather, that you had both decided?"

Once again we were witnessing the concept of abortion on demand. It was just a question of whether or not we had decided — not him, the doctor, as stipulated by law.

Sue: "Yes, I think it was, don't you?"

Litchfield: "Yes."

We were throwing out words like "we think", which should have shown that we were open to persuasion. Is it asking too much for someone to spare a little time and effort in the cause of saving a baby's life?

Dr. Chisholm: "I mean, if you feel there's any doubt at all about it, I'll leave the smear over for next time and just do the ordinary internal examination. Would you prefer me to do that?"

Sue: "Yes."

Dr. Chisholm: "Yes, right."

Sue: "I wasn't quite expecting to be examined today."

Dr. Chisholm: "Um... well, I don't quite know."

Sue: "I mean only because I came in with the sample and it was unexpected."

Dr. Chisholm: "I don't quite know whether you want me to go ahead and recommend termination?"

Sue: "Yes."

Dr. Chisholm: "I don't know about the time factor, you

see. The only way I can determine your actual date of pregnancy, the number of weeks of pregnancy, is by examination. And then... um... other things being equal, and I think at the present moment everything indicates that it's an unhappy moment for you to go on with the pregnancy... therefore, rather than leave you without help, we would recommend termination, and I would today."

Litchfield: "There couldn't be any problem with that, could there?"

Dr. Chisholm: "I don't consider so, but... er... you know it's really a matter of how possible it is for you to go on. I mean, our view is that if you're in difficulty about it and it's going to be a serious problem to you to have a child now and possibly lead, you know, to difficulties for a future child, in the sense of an unwanted child under the circumstances, then it's better, if it's at an early stage, that you should have a termination done properly, medically.

"And then start your pregnancy later when you want to. But... um... we always, of course, leave it open, even if it seems absolutely essential at the time when we do decide that termination is indicated, so anyone is, thereafter, open to decide against it."

Litchfield: "I think what Joy meant was that, if you do an examination today and she afterwards decided not to go through with a termination, nothing would be damaged by the examination?"

Dr. Chisholm: "Oh, no, no, no. But I think if you were thinking you were not going to have a termination, I think it would be probably better not to do the smear. Although I doubt very much if it would be likely to disturb anything. And the ordinary examination won't cause any disturbance at all. So, we'll leave the smear. There's no need for it. As I say, it's only a cancer exclusion smear and we can do that the next time you come. But... um... I think it's desirable first of all to consider the time factor, but also that I should go ahead and prescribe you for a suitable Pill, if you want to go on the Pill, so that, if you decide to have the termination, you can start it immediately. On the day of the operation. That's what we recommend."

Sue: "Yes, a very good idea. Come out of the clinic and

start taking it that day."

Dr. Chisholm: "Well, you start taking it while you're in there, the very day of the operation. And, of course, you understand that you will need to be seen also by Mr. Naylor, I should think, or wherever you're going, to have a second examination."

Litchfield: "A private clinic, is it?"

Dr. Chisholm: "Yes, I expect that. I know the one the counsellor has arranged."

So the abortion had already been fixed and set up *even before* Sue had been examined, or had been seen or questioned by a doctor, and even before she had decided positively to have an abortion.

"I notice she (the counsellor) has got a note here for you to see Mr. Naylor, possibly on Thursday evening," Dr. Chisholm went on. "Well, then you see it really turns on how many weeks you're pregnant, although you can't be much more than eight weeks, I should have thought. But the earlier it's done, the better."

Sue: "It's an easier operation earlier, is it?"

Dr. Chisholm: "Well, it's much less... the safety factor... the earlier it's done, the safer it is."

Sue: "Who will actually do the operation?"

Dr. Chisholm: "I don't know. It might be Mr. Naylor."

Sue: "He's a gynaecologist?"

Dr. Chisholm: "Yes, yes. It depends where it's going to be done and under what arrangements. I don't really have much to do with that. I'm simply here to make an assessment of things."

I think it is fair to suggest that all the assessments had been left to us!

Dr. Chisholm continued: "I'm here to prescribe the Pill for you, but... um... if you'd like to wait outside while I do the examination..." He was looking at Litchfield, who left the room.

"You just found out today, did you?" Dr. Chisholm asked Sue.

Sue: "Yes."

Dr. Chisholm: "But you must have felt that it was likely you were pregnant, did you?"

102

Sue: "Well, I've had the queasiness, but then, of course, you can never be sure that it isn't due to something you've eaten."

Dr. Chisholm: "Oh, no, no. That's quite true, yes. Well, I'm not going to use a speculum to examine you, so that it's only just doing the internal examination, and that doesn't disturb anything. But if you were quite certain that you're going to have a termination, I would have done a smear at the same time... The test was done here, was it?"

Sue: "Yes, this morning."

The examination was carried out swiftly.

"I don't think this can be as long as you think it is," he commented.

Sue: "How long?"

Dr. Chisholm: "Four weeks, five, perhaps six."

Just how could so many qualified doctors examine Sue internally and all pronounce her pregnant, when we know very well that she had never been expectant in her life, each one declaring a totally different stage of pregnancy? Strange — or even sinister — you might well think. One accident, one mistaken diagnosis, might be acceptable and excusable. But every time, everywhere, is too much to be fobbed off as sheer coincidence, or shoddy workmanship.

"What do you feel for, the uterus itself?" Sue inquired.

Dr. Chisholm: "Yes, the uterus itself, by the size of it. Yes, about six weeks, I think, certainly not more."

Sue: "Well, I know that you can miss periods for emotional reasons, etc."

Dr. Chisholm: "But the fact that you're getting a positive pregnancy test... Unless one can make out the top of the uterus clearly, one can't determine the size, and I'm a bit doubtful about this... I think you're going to see Mr. Naylor, aren't you?"

Sue: "Yes. It's the shape of the uterus that determines the duration?"

Dr. Chisholm: "If you can understand that the uterus gets larger as the pregnancy progresses. Therefore, if one can feel the top of the uterus clearly, one can then determine how high up it is relative to the pelvis, and that's how one judges. But as I'm not really able to feel clearly the top of the uterus, I can't determine that. It seems to me that you can't be more than a few weeks pregnant."

Sue, laughing, said: "I definitely am pregnant, am I?"

"Well, it's rather difficult to be absolutely sure, I must confess. But, if the test is positive, then I feel there's not much doubt about it."

Dr. Chisholm then recalled Litchfield.

"Er... would you like, anyway, for me to prescribe the Pill?" asked Dr. Chisholm.

"Yes, please," said Sue.

Dr. Chisholm: "I think... would you mind waiting outside and I'll see if I can have a word with the counsellor because I haven't had a chance to have a word with her?"

Sue left the room for several minutes until told to return, when Dr. Chisholm was speaking on the telephone. He was saying: "I'm not happy that I'm getting the height of the... although the test is positive, there is a chance she might not be. I was trying to contact the counsellor, but she's gone, unfortunately.

"Mr. Naylor, the gynaecologist, is coming in this evening and will be able to see you at 5.15, if you could manage to do that?" he said, posing the question to Sue.

Sue: "Yes, that's fine."

Dr. Chisholm: "So, I think I'll just leave the whole matter over for him and if that would be convenient to you, he can have another look at you. I think I'd be happier about that and he can take it from that point, you see. And if you then have time to think about it and decide to have... um... if he's quite sure about your being pregnant and you feel that you want and need a termination, then I'm sure he could do something to arrange this for you."

Litchfield: "When can the forms be signed?"

Dr. Chisholm: "Well, I think he would do that. He could arrange that all right."

Litchfield: "We were told that we had to get two signatures?"

Dr. Chisholm: "Yes, but you haven't quite made up your mind yet, have you?"

Litchfield, to Sue: "Well, you had really, hadn't you?"

Sue; "I had actually, yes. Talking to the counsellor made

me realise it would be very difficult."

Dr. Chisholm: "Yes, that's why it was a pity I couldn't have a word with her."

Litchfield: "Well, she made it clear that it was not advisable."

Sue: "Not in my situation. I think it would be the most sensible thing to do."

Litchfield, to Sue: "I think you would be happier, wouldn't you, if you could get it done as quickly as possible? I can see delays and we will have to keep coming up to town."

Dr. Chisholm: "I think what I should do is prescribe your Pills so that you can start on the day of the termination, if that's decided on, and that will save time...

"And, of course, you must not be having intercourse for a month after the operation and you would need to carry out precautions into the second packet...

"Sister will go over all this with you and I shall, meanwhile, write a little note for Mr. Naylor and, perhaps, I will give him a certificate requesting termination, in case he decides he needs a second signature.

"Is that what you... you're fairly certain in your mind... is essential?"

Sue: "Oh, yes. I had thought it all out beforehand."

Dr. Chisholm: "You really feel it's quite impossible to go on with the pregnancy?"

Sue: "Oh, yes."

Dr. Chisholm: "What would be the consequences of your going on with the pregnancy, if it is so?"

Sue: "In what sense?"

Dr. Chisholm: "Why do you regard it as impossible and essential to have a termination?"

Litchfield: "I'm married... I don't know whether..."

Dr. Chisholm: "I see..."

Sue: "But not to me."

Dr. Chisholm: "Yes, well that seems to be a very good reason. All right, if you would just go to the sister now... I have to go off to another clinic..."

The same evening, we were seen by Mr. Christopher Hardy Naylor, the gynaecologist, who also has a Harley

Street practice.

Mr. Naylor, a square-shaped man, with a bushy ginger beard, and bald, shiny head, had the abortion form, signed by Dr. Chisholm, in front of him on his desk.

Dr. Chisholm, despite expressing shades of doubt about whether or not Sue was, in fact, pregnant, had nevertheless signed a form authorising an abortion! Dr. Chisholm had started off by pronouncing Sue "four, five or six weeks" pregnant. Then, he became doubtful, unsure, but still he consented to an abortion. How can one prescribe an abortion when one is not even sure that there is a pregnancy?

Mr. Naylor, middle-aged and softly-spoken, said: "Would you like to take a seat? You'd like to be considered for a termination, is that it? I'm sure you've been through this a lot with Dr. Chisholm and and the counsellor. Can you tell me what the final conclusion is, as to why you would like to have this done?"

Sue: "Well, yes, as I've explained already, I'm not married and... um..."

Mr. Naylor: "Are you going to get married?"

Sue: "No, he's married and..."

Litchfield: "It's not really the right time is it?"

Sue: "No, it's you know..."

Mr. Naylor: "Yes, well, you'd have to cope on your own?"

Sue: "Exactly."

Mr. Naylor: "And you support her in this, do you? You think it's a good idea?"

Litchfield: "Oh, yes, I would support her in anything, anyway. But I work as well, of course."

Mr. Naylor: "Yes."

Litchfield: "And we just came to this conclusion. We discussed it and this is what we have decided."

Mr. Naylor, to Sue: "Well, I'd like to examine you and see what size the womb is, and then you (Litchfield) can come back and we'll discuss this."

Litchfield once again left the surgery, while yet another internal examination took place on Sue.

"I think Dr. Chisholm had difficulty deciding,"

commented Mr. Naylor. "Do you and your boyfriend live together, or what?"

Sue: "Well, during the week, yes."

Mr. Naylor: "Yes, well, I'll do this on Monday. Will that be all right?"

Sue: "Yes, fine."

Mr. Naylor: "And then at weekends he goes home?"

Sue: "Yes."

Mr. Naylor: "Okay, well, then, I think Monday would be the best time, because, when you come out of hospital, you need a little emotional support. And if he's around Tuesday, Wednesday, Thursday, Friday, it's the sort of remorse people get. This is, in fact, the worst thing about it all."

Sue: "Really? Why do they get remorse?"

Mr. Naylor: "For the same reason that a woman who has a miscarriage gets remorse."

Sue: "Can it be very emotionally upsetting?"

Mr. Naylor: "Yes. You need someone to help you over the next few days."

Sue: "It would be better not to be on my own then?"

Mr. Naylor: "Yes."

Sue: "How far gone am I actually?"

Mr. Naylor: "Six or eight weeks."

By this time, the phantom pregnancies had become almost mundane news. Litchfield was recalled and Mr. Naylor continued:

"Now, I think this is the sensible thing to do. I've just warned her that the most difficult thing she'll face is the feeling that can be described only as remorse or grief after it's been done. And, therefore, if you're only around during the week, let's do this on Monday. She'll spend Monday night at the hospital and you can collect her on Tuesday morning and you'll have the rest of the week together So you can help her through this."

Litchfield: "Yes, why does this feeling of remorse occur?"

Mr. Naylor: "Why does it happen? Oh, any woman who has a miscarriage or termination of pregnancy goes through this. And its intensity and severity depend on how strongly

107

motivated she is to have the termination. And I think Dr. Chisholm felt that there was some, perhaps a little ambivalence or ambience about your motivation, although you've convinced me that you're both sure."

Litchfield: "Yes, and there's no problem about having it done?"

Mr. Naylor: "No."

Litchfield: "The reason is good enough?"

Mr. Naylor: "Yes."

Sue: "And it will be done next Monday?"

Mr. Naylor: "And, of course, it will be £61. You come to my hospital and I shall do it. You'll have a consultant anaesthetist giving the anaesthetic, and you'll stay that night in hospital."

Litchfield: "When do you want the money by?"

Mr. Naylor: "When she comes in. Unless you want to give me a cheque now. Whichever suits you best."

Sue: "We'll give you cash."

Mr. Naylor: "Give me cash, yes."

Sue: "Which hospital will it be?"

Mr. Naylor: "Acton Hospital, Gunnersbury Lane, London, W.3. Whereabouts do you live?"

This was the first time he had touched on our background. We were floating false stories, false names and false addresses, but no attempt was made to verify our statements.

Mr. Naylor: "If you come in on Monday, don't have anything to eat or drink from midnight on Sunday. Try to arrive between half-past nine and ten."

Litchfield: "How far advanced is the pregnancy?"

Mr. Naylor: "Six to eight weeks."

Litchfield: "She was apprehensive because we didn't know if we had sufficient grounds for an abortion."

Mr. Naylor: "Oh, that was the explanation. All right... yes, I understand. Well, you see, the grounds depend on how one interprets the law. I think you have sufficient grounds.

"If you want to ring me, you can always get me at Harley Street in the evenings, but if you want to discuss the arrangements for admission or anything like that, talk to my secretary, who's at the Central Middlesex Hospital. (He handed over his personal card). And that's the letter you bring when you come to the hospital (he gave us a letter). And I'd like to see you back here in three weeks' time. So could you make an appointment?"

Sue: "What time will the operation be done?"

Mr. Naylor: "Two o'clock, and you come down to the operating theatre, have an injection into the vein and go to sleep. And while you're asleep, very gently I stretch the neck of the womb and, using a suction process, which is the best and the most modern, I remove the embryonic tissue, and the womb closes back. You go back to the ward, you wake up and you can have some tea.

"You must stay in one night, in case you have a haemorrhage or an infection. But I don't anticipate any problems, because you've come early on in the pregnancy and it should be straightforward."

The letter Mr. Naylor had given us was addressed to "Sister, Lady Skinner Ward, Acton Hospital, Gunnersbury Lane, London, W.3." We kept the letter and all documents, including the totally completed abortion form.

Mr. Naylor spoke of the "remorse", the "grief" and the "emotional" dangers following an abortion. He said that Sue should not be left alone after being discharged from hospital. You cannot experience remorse without knowing that you have done something wrong. Grief following an abortion can only mean that the woman realises that she has lost a child that was living, not something inanimate or unalive, and she is in mourning; self-induced mourning. In public, the pro-abortionists are conspicuously silent about things such as "remorse", "grief" and "emotional traumas". They advocate that a girl should have an abortion because there is no one to give her support. But then, when she arrives for the operation, she is told that it is dangerous unless she has someone to be with her continuously after the abortion, because of the "remorse, grief and emotion". The reason she is there is because there is no one to whom she can turn. So, by the gynaecologists' own admission and by a girl's own circumstance, she is being placed in severe mental and physical danger by having an abortion.

Why is there so much silence on this aspect of abortion? All the so-called pregnancy "advisory" services continually reassured us that there was nothing to an abortion. "It's not really an operation at all," was common propaganda. "You can return to work the very next day," Sue was always being told. Then, from Mr. Naylor, we begin to learn something of the frightening truth about the way girls are often blinkered, blindfolded and fooled to enable affluent men to become even richer.

Pregnant and frightened girls are lured, coaxed and snared into a net that holds so many dangers, both mental and physical.

"It's hectic all the time — we never stop"

The Avenue Clinic, 14, New Church Road, Hove, Sussex, has nothing whatsoever to do with charity. Of that, there is no doubt. It features in this section because it was this clinic that served as a stepping-stone on our way to Wiston's, Brighton, which is part of the British Pregnancy Advisory Service group, whose headquarters are in Birmingham.

The Avenue Clinic, Hove, is owned by Mr. Immanuel Bierer, who is well-known in international abortion circles. He also owns a private abortion clinic of the same name in North London, and he has offices in Harley Street, next door to Dr. Shoham's surgery.

When we arrived at the Avenue Clinic, Hove, Sue said that she believed she was pregnant and wanted to know if they would do an abortion for her.

One of the staff said that she would send for a senior nurse. While we were waiting in a small office, Litchfield said: "Busy time for you, is it?"

"Hectic all the time," said the woman.

"You work nights as well?" Litchfield asked.

"Yes, I should think today they'll be in the theatre all night."

Sue: "You do a lot of terminations, do you?"

Woman: "Mostly general surgery. We do a few each day, you know, if it's there, we don't sort of... we've got one or two doctors who come here. The deputy matron will advise you to go to see one of them."

While waiting for Miss Bell, the Deputy Matron, we admired a painting of Jesus Christ carrying the Cross.

Miss Bell entered briskly, asking: "Hello, can I help you?"

She was smartly-dressed and wore more than a modicum

of make-up. Miss Bell, in her thirties, sat at her desk below a chart showing the timetable of theatre duties and operations.

"I think I'm pregnant and I wanted to try to get a termination," said Sue.

"Are you from Brighton?" Miss Bell queried.

"Yes." said Sue.

Miss Bell: "Well what I can suggest to you is to try Mr. Measday. I'll, perhaps, 'phone him, and, obviously, you'll have to go and see him."

Sue: "What is he, a doctor?"

Miss Bell: "A gynaecologist. He comes to us. But, as I say, you know... we don't have anyone on the premises. Wiston's — have you been to Wiston's at all?"

Sue: "No."

Miss Bell: "Well, that is another place. Obviously, you have to go and you have to be screened and all this sort of thing, but they'll probably do it for you in a few days or a week. So, it's just up to you really. Whether you want it done privately or at Wiston's."

Sue: "Wiston's is not a private place, then?"

Miss Bell: "Not altogether. Obviously the fee varies considerably."

Litchfield: "Best done privately, I suppose, isn't it?"

Miss Bell: "Well, it's up to you. I don't really think it makes a lot of difference. We do a few terminations here, but it's not purely terminations. Wiston's is — that's all they do. But it's just up to you. By all means, I'll phone Mr. Measday and see if I can fit an appointment for you."

Sue: "Yes, have you any idea what it would cost?"

Miss Bell: "Yes, well it depends, obviously, how far you are, but it's from £100 to £105. That's inclusive."

Litchfield: "That's all right. Will it take long to get arranged?"

Miss Bell: "No, no. It's the bed state at the moment..." She studied the wall-chart. "Um... it should probably be better next Monday, Tuesday, as far as we're concerned with the bed situation," she added.

Litchfield: "How long would she have to be in?"

Miss Bell: "Have to be overnight. But it's a matter of

coming in, you know, you only need come in two or three hours beforehand because you have to have blood taken. And then you have it done. It's only a matter of what... ten, ten or fifteen minutes, something like that Then you have to stay overnight. That's the law."

Litchfield: "There shouldn't be any problems to get it done?"

Miss Bell: "No, not at all. So would you like me to phone Mr. Measday?" She was assuring us of an abortion without having asked us *one* question regarding our circumstances or reasons for seeking a termination.

We said that we would like her to contact Mr. Measday for us. Litchfield then asked the all-important question: "Do we have to give reasons why we want a termination?"

"No," said Miss Bell, "It's purely your private reasons It's nothing to do with anybody else. And it's up to you to tell them if you want. Well, that's entirely up to you."

This was possibly the most shameful and scandalous lie of the whole inquiry. Here was the deputy matron of a clinic aiding us to break the law. It *is* the Government's business to know that abortions are being performed only for the reasons stipulated in the Act. It is *not* a private matter. The Government has to be informed why each abortion is being carried out. A woman is required by law to justify her claims for a legal abortion. She has no right, as falsely and misleadingly intimated by Miss Bell, to keep her grounds secret. Each case, by law, should be vetted and scrutinised by two doctors, both acting in "good faith".

Litchfield: "I just wondered whether we had to have a reason?"

Miss Bell: "No, no."

This was symptomatic of the whole private abortion sector we encountered. We were paying to circumnavigate the law. People in the trade have become desensitised by time and the sheer number of abortions It is not just a question of "turning a blind eye". Illegal abortions in the sense that they are done without just cause, have become so commonplace that a vast number of people have even brainwashed themselves. They really *do believe* the law has decreed abortion on demand. This, however, is not the law

113

of the land. It is the law of the abortion jungle. The private sector works on the assumption that to have enough money is to have enough reason. This is their moral. This is *their* law. It is not, though, the law of Parliament. These pirates adjust their camouflage according to their location. In Harley Street, the sophistication is sickening. When you get to Hove, they are not so particular about the veneer. They do not bother to fill in the cracks and gaping holes in their façade.

"I thought there was a form to sign?" said Sue.

Miss Bell: "Well, all you sign is a consent form to agree. And there are forms that we have to fill in, that Mr. Measday has to fill in."

Litchfield: "But we don't have to bother about that?"

Miss Bell: "No. They'll tell you. All we have to do, all you have to do, is sign a consent form. That's for the anaesthetic."

Sue: "The normal operation form you sign? The one where you give the next of kin?"

Miss Bell, laughing: "Yes, it's just all these formalities." Then she telephoned Mr. Measday.

"Hello, is Mr. Measday in, please?" she inquired. "Um... yes, it's Miss Bell from the Avenue Clinic. I've got a lady here about a termination. I was wondering if she could come along and see Mr. Measday. If you could make an appointment for her? Oh, yes, that'll be fine, 3.45. Pardon? No, I'm not, I'm matron of the Avenue Clinic. Oh... um... well, what number do I ring? 109. Okay, fine. Thank you very much, bye."

Turning to us, Miss Bell said: "That's okay."

Litchfield: "Who will we pay the money to?"

Miss Bell: "Normally to here and we sort it out from there."

Litchfield: "You want cash?"

Miss Bell: "Yes."

Litchfield: "I was just wondering how far gone Sue is?"

Miss Bell; "Well, this will have to be for Mr. Measday to decide. I'm not quite sure up to how many weeks he'll do this, but 14 weeks is fair enough, I think. But, then, I can't speak for the surgeon who's doing it."

Sue: "It's Mr. Measday?"

Miss Bell: "Yes. He'll expect you tomorrow." She gave us a note with his address and the time and date of the appointment.

Sue: "Right, thank you very much."

Miss Bell: "We won't be able to fit you in until after the weekend. He'll let us know, anyway. Thank you, bye bye."

It was good to be out in the fresh air again...

We did not keep this appointment with Mr. Measday. Instead, we decided to see just how easy it would be to arrange an abortion with him "off-the-cuff", without being introduced by Miss Bell. We learned that Mr. Measday was operating in the afternoons at Wiston's Clinic, Hove, which, as already stated, is owned by the British Pregnancy Advisory Service. Litchfield went to Wiston's and asked to speak to Mr. Measday. Litchfield told Mr. Measday: "I want to fix up an abortion for a friend of mine. Can you help me?"

"Of course," he said. "Get her to come to my surgery tomorrow afternoon. Would 3.30 be all right?" Litchfield agreed to the abortion rendez-vous. Litchfield then explained that we wanted the abortion to be performed at the Avenue Clinic and not in Wiston's.

"That'll be okay," he said. What a bizarre and irregular situation: here was Litchfield, just having waltzed into a "charitable" clinic, chatting up a gynaecologist to do an abortion at a rival establishment!

The name Litchfield chose to use was Denton. He said that Sue's surname was Oliver.

In search of more instant information, Litchfield telephoned Mr. Measday's surgery the following morning. Mr. Measday was engaged with a patient, but the conversation with his secretary was fruitful. It went as follows:

Litchfield: "Is Mr. Measday there, please?"

Secretary: "Yes, hold on, please. Well, I'm his secretary speaking."

Litchfield: "This is Denton..."

Secretary: "You were bringing in a Mrs. Oliver, is that right?"

Litchfield: "Yes, I made an appointment."

Secretary: "For 3.30, yes."

Litchfield: "I met Mr. Measday. I had a chat with him at Wiston's..."

Secretary: "He did tell me about it."

Litchfield: "Unfortunately, I made the appointment on the spot, without being sure Miss Oliver could make it and it's impossible, because she's out of town today."

This was not so. Sue was tape-recording the entire conversation, as we did with subsequent talks with Mr. Measday.

"Could I have a word with Mr. Measday, do you think?" Litchfield asked.

Secretary: "Yes, can I make an appointment for her to come next week?"

Litchfield: "Yes, that would be fine."

Secretary: "Now, we're here on a Monday morning or, of course, a Thursday afternoon..."

Litchfield: "Well, Monday morning. I should think."

Secretary: "Monday morning. Could she be here by quarter past nine?"

Litchfield: "Yes, she could."

Secretary: "Only... fine, because, then, you know, get things going... um... I'll put her in at 9.15 on Monday morning then, Mr. Denton. You know where she's to come — 109, The Drive, Hove."

Litchfield: "I don't know whether I should have a word with Mr. Measday about it?"

Secretary: "He's examining a patient at the moment."

Litchfield: "The point is, the reason why I've approached Mr. Measday is that she wanted it done in the Avenue Clinic."

Secretary: "Yes, I gathered... I do know about the case, Mr. Denton."

Litchfield: "Do you? The reason is, well, I know Mr. Bierer in London and that is his clinic, isn't it?"

Secretary: "That's right. The Avenue, New Church Road, Hove."

Litchfield: "Does Mr. Measday want to know the stage of the pregnancy?"

Secretary: "Not before she comes. Let's hope it's not too far. That's the most important thing, of course. The sooner she comes, the better."

Litchfield: "Yes. Is there any problem about what one has to do? I believe two doctors have to sign?"

Secretary: "Yes, well, Mr. Measday can always get a colleague of his to sign the Part Two. Yes, that's all right."

Litchfield: "There shouldn't be any delay there?"

Secretary: "There shouldn't be any at all, really, no."

Litchfield: "I just wondered whether she ought to get another doctor to sign anything first, or not, to save time?"

Secretary: "Well, if she feels she'd like to. But there's always other doctors working there, you know, and working with Mr. Measday. Because, of course, it's not only he that is involved. There's the anaesthetist and the pathologist. There's plenty of doctors. They're well looked after."

Litchfield: "She's just a bit worried about whether she's got sufficient grounds. I think you have to have a reason, don't you?"

Secretary: "Well, usually, it's a start that she's unmarried... I take it? I don't think she should have any problems. But, of course, it is a thing that has to be decided with the consultant."

Litchfield: "Yes, well, that was why I wanted a word with him."

Secretary: "Well, I think, as I say, they'll sort that out all right and if she comes Monday morning, I gather she'll, obviously, want to get on with it straight away. So she might even have the op. on Monday afternoon."

Litchfield: "Well, that's fine, so I'll tell her to come prepared?"

Secretary: "Oh, I should, yes."

Litchfield: "What, should she just bring an overnight bag?"

Secretary: "Yes, 'cos they're usually discharged after twenty-four hours."

Litchfield: "You'll want her to pay in cash?"

Secretary: "I'm afraid that is the arrangement, yes."

Litchfield: "How much will it be?"

Secretary: "It's £100. That covers everybody, you see. The nursing home, and Mr. Measday, and the anaesthetist and the... it all sounds a lot, but, by the time they get their little bit, you know..."

Litchfield: "Yes, it's all got to be shared out, hasn't it?"

Secretary: "Yes, it has."

Litchfield: "Anyway, you don't think there's any reason for her to worry that she won't get it done?"

Secretary: "Obviously, it's not for me to say definitely, one hundred percent, but a jolly good ninety-nine, I would say. I mustn't commit myself all the way, of course, but I don't think she need worry."

Litchfield: "There's nothing that she should particularly say?"

Secretary: "No, it's sorted out. I'm afraid she's not the first young lady by any manner (laughing). Tell her not to worry too much. She'll be well looked after there."

Litchfield: "And the fact that she isn't married ought to be enough?"

Secretary: "Well, it's a good start, anyway (laughing again). Okay, tell her not to worry. We'll see her Monday morning. Bye bye. Thank you for ringing."

The same evening, we telephoned Mr. Measday, at his home. He is another middle-aged man, built squarely and dresses like a door-to-door salesman. His speech is placid, even, and he has the mark of taciturnity.

"Good evening," said Sue. "You won't know me. My name is Miss Oliver. Mr. Denton spoke to you."

"Ah, yes!" Mr. Measday interjected.

"I'm sorry to bother you at home, but I wanted to ask you whether it was all right..."

Mr. Measday: "Oh, yes. It should be perfectly all right. I understood you were coming to see me on Monday?"

Sue: "That's right. I'm sorry I couldn't make the appointment today, but I didn't know of the arrangements in time."

Mr. Measday: "Oh, that's quite all right."

Sue: "I understand it will be all right for me to bring my overnight things on Monday?"

Mr. Measday: "Yes, I believe my secretary telephoned

the Avenue Clinic and I believe that you are, sort of, known there, or have approached them yourself, have you not?"

Sue: "Well, Mr. Denton knows Mr. Bierer, the owner."

Mr. Measday: "I see, yes. Yes, of course. Yes, it's fine by me. I can organise it."

Sue had not even been examined by *one* doctor, let alone two, and Mr. Measday, the gynaecologist, was *promising* to fix the abortion. Reasons, and so forth, just did not enter into the discussion.

Sue: "And will you examine me?"

Mr. Measday: "Yes. I forget what time you are coming."

Sue: "I don't actually know, but I am sure Mr. Denton does."

Mr. Measday: "I can't remember, but I saw it in the book. It will be mid-morning, I think. And you'll go straight from me, I imagine, to the nursing home and get settled in."

Sue: "And the operation would be later in the day?"

Mr. Measday: "That's right. In the afternoon."

Sue: "What about signing the form, or whatever it is?"

Mr. Measday: "Well, I shall on your behalf, as one of the signatures and I will find... one of my colleagues will do the other."

Sue: "I was rather worried because I don't know how one qualifies, or whether being private, this doesn't matter?"

Mr. Measday, clearing his throat: "Well, it's very difficult, of course. One cannot officially promise anything until one has seen you. But... um... generally speaking... er... the law is interpreted so widely nowadays that, really, it's not very difficult to rake up reasons to justify it."

Sue: "Exactly. And if I say I'm not married, you see?"

Mr. Measday: "Yes, most people would accept that, you know, as a good enough choice on your part when you are sufficiently early, as you are."

Sue: "Yes, precisely. Thank you very much. There was one other thing. The money side of it; did you want cash or a cheque?"

Mr. Measday: "Well (clearing his throat again), it's easier in a way if you can bring cash. The thing being that four people are paid with it. So you could pay with four cheques, if you prefer."

Sue: "Who would I have to make out the cheques to?"

Mr. Measday: "Well, that depends a little bit on who does your blood test, and I expect I know the anaesthetist, but until I organise it... you'd have to sign it, if you would, at the time. Or put in the names at the time."

Sue: "And yourself and the other doctor?"

Mr. Measday: "Yes, and the Avenue Clinic itself."

Sue: "So there would be cheques for two doctors, the Avenue Clinic and the anaesthetist?"

Mr. Measday: "That's right. That's right. Four in all."

Sue: "But I will try to bring the cash, though."

Mr. Measday: "Just exactly as you wish, whichever is the most convenient."

Sue: "And it is £100, is it?"

Mr. Measday: "That's right, yes. I'll look forward to seeing you on Monday. Goodbye."

It is almost beyond belief: we had casually, nonchalantly sauntered into an abortion clinic, and unannounced and completely unknown, spoken to a gynaecologist and negotiated with him to perform a termination for us in another nursing home. In all reputable territories of medicine, patients have to be referred by their own doctor to a specialist. You cannot just bump into them on the pavement or passing through a door and say, "Hey, mate, can you do a job on a girl for me sometime." This is what we did and it seemed to be nothing uncommon. Mr. Measday appeared throughout to be very pleased and eager to do business.

. . . .

Wiston's, the BPAS clinic in Hove, has become an international centre for abortion. Girls come from all over the world on special abortion "junkets" to Wiston's. Every week chartered coaches, offering cut-price fares, leave Paris and other European cities — many from Germany — for Brighton, England, with pregnant women in search of an abortion. Each one is armed with a map of the Brighton area, with an ink circle marking the location of Wiston's Clinic.

Before leaving home, all the girls pay a visit to their bank and draw out the necessary cash for the operation. Many of the women take their husbands or boyfriends with them, combining an abortion with a weekend holiday or a miniature tour of Britain. In fact, there was something of this carnival mood and merriment reflected at Wiston's.

Many boarding houses have been making a fortune in the neighbourhood of Wiston's. While the wife or girlfriend is having an abortion and spending one night in the clinic, the husbands and boyfriends are taking refuge with some of the infamous landladies of Brighton.

"The holiday season lasts only from July until September," said one landlady. "There is no abortion season. It's just as busy all the year round. Every day throughout the year is a Bank Holiday for us now. We are banking money every day! We don't bother with holidaymakers any more. The ones we deal with are all foreigners. Right mugs they are, too! I can charge them what I like and get away with it. Thank God for the Abortion Act. I don't know what we would do without it. So many people take holidays abroad, the bottom has gone out of the holiday trade for the private guest house."

Since taking over Wiston's, an old, well-established nursing home, BPAS has added extensions, in addition to modernising the vintage part. The reception areas resemble the customs' hall at an international airport. Women drift from desk to desk. "No Smoking" instructions are spelt in several different languages. The machine-gun like chatter and clatter of a host of foreign tongues reverberates from wall to wall.

In a "lounge" equipped with a television set, men sat with suitcases and zipper-bags by their feet. The girls in the reception area all spoke foreign languages, including French and German.

Outside, Litchfield spoke to a number of Frenchmen who had brought their wives to Wiston's for abortions. "We're going out on the town now," said one of them. "We have booked a few escort girls for the evening and we are going to take them out to dinner. We've been looking forward to this trip for a week or so now. It's the third time I've been to England, but it's my wife's first abortion. Perhaps we'll be back again — if I can get my wife pregnant again!"

Another said: "I don't agree with what my wife is doing, but I allowed her to make up her own mind. I thought they might try to make her see reason at the clinic, but, instead, they just treated the whole thing as a joke. I think it is a bit sick myself. I'm in two minds about going back on my own and leaving my wife to make her own way back to France — if she wants to. This place is terrible. They've lost all sense of decency and respect. Even the landlady at the boarding house said: 'You've got the abortion suite tonight.' She has four men in each room every night, she told us. The house is packed.

"The landlady joked that she gives young married couples the bridal suite and at the same time books them into the abortion suite for three months hence. It's not very funny, is it?"

No, I agree, it is not very funny.

When we subjected Wiston's to closer scrutiny, we went to the reception desk, where a girl said: "Can I help you?"

"I have an appointment for 11 o'clock this morning," Sue replied. We had made an advance appointment. "I wasn't quite clear who it would be with?" Sue continued.

"Well, you see two doctors, then you see the almoner and then they'll tell you when you're coming in."

Sue had not even been declared pregnant by a doctor at the clinic. She had not undergone one examination. No grounds for a possible abortion had been discussed, and yet the staff were talking about *"when you're coming in."*

Throughout this gutter industry, we found that cases were continually being pre-judged, simply because *real* reasons were never required in the private sector.

Litchfield was instructed to sit in the "lounge" while Sue was seen by a clerk. The dialogue went as follows:

Clerk: "Have you had your pregnancy test confirmed by a urine test here?"

Sue: "Yes, I brought one last Wednesday."

This was true and the result had been... yes, yet again... POSITIVE.

Clerk: "Are you Miss or Mrs.?"

Sue: "Mrs."

Clerk: "And the address we can write to?"

Sue gave a false address — a Brighton one which could quite easily have been checked out to determine its validity or otherwise.

Clerk: "Have you been to see your doctor?"

Sue: "No."

Clerk: "Leave him out of it, will we? Now have you had a cancer smear test taken before?"

Sue: "Yes."

Clerk: "Your date of birth, and have you got your medical card with you?"

Sue: "May 16, 1946. No, I forgot my medical card."

Clerk: "When you come in for your operation, perhaps you could bring it or ring up your doctor's secretary and just ask her for it."

Sue: "What do you want to know this for?"

Clerk: "I think, possibly, we have to submit records to the Ministry, in actual fact, of how many terminations we carry out and, I think, it's just this little double check that we're carrying out... the terminations we say we've carried out. You know, just something official. You're living with your husband, are you?"

Sue: "Yes."

Clerk: "What is your age?"

Sue: "Twenty-seven."

Clerk: "Can I have £10 now, please?"

Sue, handing over the £10: "How much is the abortion?"

Clerk: "£61. £10 now and then £51 when you come for your operation."

Sue: "I see, the £10 goes towards it?"

Clerk: "Yes."

Sue: "And how soon could I get it done?"

Clerk: "Well, within ten days, certainly."

Sue: "And it's an overnight stay, is it?"

Clerk: "Yes, 24 hours in the nursing home. This will all

be explained to you this afternoon."

Sue: "What about reasons?"

Clerk: "Reasons? Well, the social worker you'll see first will ask you why you want a termination and then the doctors will take the medical side of it. In actual fact, it's a doctors' decision. But, if you're pretty certain this is what you want... perhaps you've had your family have you?"

Sue: "I haven't had a family at all."

Clerk: "No, you don't want a family yet? Well, you tell them this and they'll help you about it."

After this initial interview, Sue had to wait ninety minutes before being sent upstairs to the social workers' anteroom, where she observed a girl in her early twenties, an office clerk, rapidly filling in and stamping the official green abortion forms with doctors' names BEFORE the patients had seen the medical staff.

"You seem to have no end of paper work there, don't you become bored with it?" said Sue, making conversation.

"Not really," the girl replied, "I reckon I could do it in my sleep now. I can keep on the line without looking." The girl was referring to the doctors' official stamp on the abortion form which is not supposed, by law, to be there until after the examination and when it has been officially decided that there is ample grounds for a termination.

"Have you done mine yet?" asked Sue.

Girl: *"Yes."*

Sue: "How do you know which is mine?"

Girl: "Well, I guessed, because you're the only English one." Sue then found the abortion form containing her name. On it was stamped the names and addresses of two doctors before she had been seen by them.

Girl: "Those are the two doctors you will see this afternoon."

The girl was penned in her desk by seven large brown cartons containing files on women who had undergone abortions. A further fourteen cartons were piled high in an adjacent room.

Ahead of Sue in the queue to see the counsellors were an assortment of nationalities — two French girls, a German and a Chinese, who was unable to speak a word of English.

124

A squabble broke out between two counsellors who were cursing because no one could communicate with the Chinese girl.

"Just push her through and get her done," said one official. "She's here for an abortion not a debate."

It was then Sue's turn to see the counsellor.

Counsellor: "That's your receipt for the £10. You hang on to it."

Sue: "I believe that you want another £51."

Counsellor: "That's when you book for the day to have your operation. We do it in two bits, just in case you decide you don't want to go ahead." She then referred to a two-page questionnaire.

"You sound sure, anyway," she laughed. "Now, if there's anything you're worried about or anything you want to know, just ask."

Sue: "What happens this afternoon?"

Counsellor: "Well, what happens is this. I'm a counsellor, and I'm here to put your mind at rest. And any worries you've got or any problems we can help you with, fair enough. And then you have to see two doctors. One gives you an internal examination and askes medical questions, and takes a drop of blood. We've got our own blood bank here and yours will be cross-matched, ready if needed for the operation. Now, it's not on demand, but they're very sympathetic. Only if you're much too large, or it's a very flippant reason, such as you want to go on holiday, you can't be bothered, or anything like that...

"Now the whole two forms are quite confidential. They go into medical records which are kept here only. There's rather a lot of questions, but they're all of a physical nature. In no way do we moralise. This is not our job at all.

"Purely physical. The doctor takes off what he wants on here and then he asks his medical questions, and they are just put into a computer, which we keep. So, if by some unlikely chance, you had to come back again, we've got your records here. Now, first of all, when did you make the appointment? Today? How long have we kept you waiting?"

Sue: "Three days ago."

Counsellor: "Oh, fine. Gosh! We are up-to-date. Now, have you been to your own doctor?"

Sue: "No."

Counsellor: "And you don't wish to?"

Sue: "No."

Counsellor: "That's quite all right. Only, when you've had your op... in six weeks' time, will you come back to us for a check-up? And you won't be kept waiting, because there's no counselling. You just go in and see the doctor."

Sue: "Yes, you do seem terribly busy today."

Counsellor: "Well, not really. Yesterday morning, we had nineteen up here. We do thirty abortions a day, seven days a week. And there's two counsellors working always. And this is the difficulty. This is why we try to find out how long we've kept you waiting. I mean, we feel a week is quite long enough... Now is this your husband's child by any chance?"

Sue: "Yes. Tell me, why do I have to see two doctors?"

Counsellor: "Because it is the law that the termination form has two doctors' signatures on it. You see, if you go to your own doctor and explain, and he's sympathetic, he has got abortion forms as well. He will sign the first part of it for you and then you only have to see one doctor here. But, by law, there has to be two. But you don't have two examinations. The other usually just says you are quite sure about this.

"Er... mainly because you have got, say, half married people and half youngsters coming here and we don't want anyone, even if they are sixteen, to be pushed into having this done if they don't want to. And this second doctor is really an extra safeguard, you see?"

Sue: "Will one of these doctors actually do it?"

Counsellor: "Oh, no, you will have a gynaecologist do the op. These are referral doctors. They are all local doctors...

"And this probably seems a silly question, but what religion were you born to? You don't still have to have it?"

Sue: "I'm Church of England."

Counsellor: "Why we ask is in case you are Roman Catholic. We have a lot of Roman Catholics and some of them are upset religiously. And we actually have a parson who can see them. But this isn't going to perturb you?"

Sue: "No. He (the parson) would explain the reasons to them why it was all right to go ahead with the abortion?"

Counsellor: "Well, yes, if they're going to be in such a state of guilt and trauma, you see...

"Did you get sex-education at school. Not worms and rabbits?"

Sue: "No."

Counsellor: "I think it's something that is fairly new, don't you? You've had a urine test here, haven't you? Well, we know it's accurate, then. It doesn't seem to be quite so much over here, only foreign girls have a do-it-yourself kit which is quite unsafe. You get negatives that are wrong and positives that are wrong. Have you any other children?"

Sue: "No, I haven't any children."

Counsellor: "Never had a miscarriage or an abortion?"

Sue: "No, I've never been pregnant."

Counsellor: "Do you want any children or not?"

Sue: "Not at the moment, no."

Counsellor: "Now, why we ask how many children you hope to have in a family, if any, is that we do want to assure you that this will not stop you having children in the future. I don't know if you've heard that you can become sterile from an abortion? Well, if you go into a dirty, back-street, yes, you get infected, but not here."

These are scandalous lies. Women become sterile after having abortions in the "best" clinics. Infections also occur after such operations. Sterility and infections are not confined to the back-streets. The counsellor should have talked in terms of relativity and percentages, to have been honest and fair.

The counsellor, laughing, went on: "But what it will do is probably make you more fertile, so, please, be very careful."

This is another myth which has been disproved. This counsellor was a fountain of erroneous knowledge.

"They're so sure about this that all the doctors who work here... these referral doctors who'll see you are very well up on all forms of contraception and they'll be more

127

than happy to discuss this with you, if you wish it?

"Only, we don't force this on you at all. If you'd rather go to your own doctor or Family Planning, okay. But you are likely to be more fertile and we don't want to see you back again.

"We're still willing to have you back. Don't feel you can't, but, on the other hand, we don't want you to become pregnant if possible."

Sue: "Would it do any harm to have more than one?"

Counsellor: "No, it certainly wouldn't. But you are taking a risk, in the sense, my dear, that any operation is a risk. A slight risk. But certainly, if you made a mistake... You're under anaesthetic. And we don't want people to use it as a form of contraception. It is not a good thing. We've had people a second time, sure. You know, it certainly can be done, but we would rather you did, you know, something else, if possible.

"Now this question, my dear, covers all your sex-life. In no way do we moralise. We just want to know what's letting you down. Now we're not being nosey. We want to know how fertile you are. Have you ever done it with no contraceptive and not become pregnant? Some people can go months or a year."

Sue: "Yes, we have sometimes."

Counsellor: "And on this occasion, it was nothing, was it?"

Sue: "That's right."

Counsellor: "Right you are. Now, have you got your National Health number?"

Sue: "I'm sorry, I forgot to bring it."

Counsellor: "Well, it doesn't matter. When you come in for your op. just bring it then, but, even if you forget it, don't let it upset you. It doesn't really matter."

Sue: "Why do you want it?"

Counsellor: "Well, the thing is, if by some chance, you should die, we've got your number. But, touch wood (she did so twice), we have got five abortion clinics and we have never lost anyone. But that is really the only reason. As I say, we are so happy about it that it doesn't really matter. Now, are you quite sure your husband's in agreement with this?"

Sue: "Yes, he is."

Counsellor: "Now we do have to put why you want it done. Now, although all these forms are confidential, this little bit only can be cut off the bottom and be shown to the Ministry, but it has no name, no address. It just states, 'this patient feels unable to continue this pregnancy because...' and we have to cover the doctors, you see. So what reason do you want it done for, then?"

Sue: "Er... what... um... what?"

Counsellor: "I mean, why do you want it terminated? Why don't you want to go ahead with it?"

Sue: "Well, I just don't want to go on with it, you know..."

Counsellor: "You don't want children full stop?"

Sue: "Well, no. It's not convenient really because my husband's building up a business at the moment and I'm helping him with it, and we hadn't planned to have a family for about four or five years."

Counsellor: "Really, it's financial. I can say that financially it's difficult at present."

Sue: "Mmm..."

Counsellor: "Your husband's your age, is he?"

Sue: "He's thirty-four."

Counsellor: "Yes, so you've just started this busines lately and, financially, it would be extremely difficult?"

Sue: "Well, it's not so much financially extremely difficult, but we would like to provide the best for children when we have them, you know."

Counsellor: "Well, may I say then, that at the present time you're building up a business and... er... you hope to have children at a later date? Okay?"

Sue: "Yes, that's it."

Counsellor: "Right, that's fine. And we like to be, you know, as honest as we can. But, you see, we've got a lot of very sympathetic doctors down here who work for us. Although we're completely legal, the Ministry of Health can walk in at any time. We have a licence, you see, that can be taken away if the slightest thing is wrong. We do have to cover the doctors.

"You'll be having a general anaesthetic, and you have to be here by 7.30 in the morning. It's just a prick in the vein or your hand. That's all there is to it. You go to sleep and you come to. It's all over and done with, and you're back in the ward. Your husband can visit you at seven in the evening, if you want him to. And the next morning, my dear, you can leave at 7.15. Now you're not chucked out, you can go and sit in the lounge if he's picking you up."

Sue: "How soon could I have it done?"

Counsellor: "Well, you'll have to see the almoner, dear. She knows the bed-bookings. As soon as the doctors have passed you through, go downstairs and she will book you in. You go in her office and you book it, and she tells you all about payment. Now look, we do work seven days a week, so if one day is more convenient, don't mind saying so.

"But you are only ten weeks pregnant, and you see, I've had three this afternoon who are bordering on sixteen weeks, and they've got to be done fairly smartish..."

Sue: "Will it be done within a week or a fortnight?"

Counsellor: "Can't tell at all. It might even be tomorrow! But I've no idea how the beds are. They fluctuate terrifically. You see, sometimes we literally get six or eight French girls over together and of course, then, you see, this does make an awful lot of difference...

"Now dear, if you would go and wait to see the doctors. I'm afraid there's a queue. You will be an hour or more."

We had discovered all that we wanted to learn about the running of Wiston's, its attitudes and its treatment of women.

An Abortion on Hire-Purchase

The London Pregnancy Advisory Service, a separate organisation from the BPAS, though in spirit they are as close as ugly sisters, is hidden from daylight in the basement of 40, Margaret Street, W.1. It is a miserable place, which some might think is befitting its station and function in society. Sue had to descend into a London basement to find this establishment.

The London Pregnancy Advisory Serice and the BPAS hold hands in their work like blood relatives. BPAS will pass girls on to LPAS, and vice-versa. It is all very chummy. This is not surprising because they both come under the rather porous umbrella of charities. The question is, of course, to whom are they charitable? Certainly not to the babies they cremate in the perversion of charity.

Sue took a sample and waited for the result; after about half an hour, she was summoned into a small office to be confronted by a counsellor.

"We've done the test and the result is POSITIVE." said the counsellor, maintaining the record of one hundred percent inaccuracy throughout the abortion clinics, testing units and pregnancy "advisory" services of Great Britain. "You were pretty well expecting that, were you?"

"Yes," said Sue dryly. The counsellor could not have deduced the real meaning in Sue's reply.

Counsellor: "Are you quite happy about it, or what?"

Sue: "Well, I wonder if you could help, actually? I don't know how many weeks that would make it?"

Counsellor: "You are roughly going to be about nine to ten weeks."

Sue: "Can anything be done at ten weeks?"

Counsellor: "You're thinking of a termination, are you?"

131

Sue: "Yes."

Counsellor: "Oh, yes, this can be done."

Sue: "I didn't know what the latest stage was?"

Counsellor: "Well, you could have a termination without any problems up to twelve weeks. Terminations can be done beyond that. Really, between thirteen and fourteen weeks, it's no problem at all. Gynaecologists do terminate up to eighteen weeks. So, you're not borderline. You've been thinking like this, have you?"

Sue: "Yes."

Counsellor: "You've got no children or...?"

Sue: "No, I'm not married."

Counsellor: "I see, yes, so you really feel that you don't want to go ahead?"

Sue: "Yes."

Counsellor: "Well, we can make an appointment for you. The unit upstairs is separate from us, but they do, sort of, make all the arrangements. You can go up to reception and book an appointment. You come back here on the day of the appointment. There's a bit of a wait at the moment, and you would see a counsellor who would just sort out with you general information and the reasons why you've decided to have a termination. That kind of thing. Then you would see the doctor who would confirm how far pregnant you are and fill in the necessary medical part of it. Then you would be referred straight away to the gynaecologist who's a Harley Street specialist, and who would book the bed at the nursing home and make all the arrangements for you.

"So, it would probably be within the week of your coming to that appointment that you would go to the nursing home, and it will be a twenty-four hour stay there."

Sue: "How much?"

Counsellor: "You would pay £7.50 consultation fee when you come here, when you would see a counsellor, the doctor and the gynaecologist. That would leave £55 to pay for the nursing home when you actually went in."

Sue: "Can I pay by cheque or...?"

Counsellor: "Well, they do like it in cash, unfortunately, because we... they... have had so many times of being let

132

down by cheques that they've had to, sort of, bring out a different ruling.

"If you have any problems about not being able to get the money all at once or at the time you see the gynaecologist, you can see the Financial Secretary who can make all arrangements. They can pay the nursing home for you and you can forward the money on afterwards. We never want to feel that the money is standing in the way if you really want to have a termination."

Sue: "I know that you have to have good reasons in law. I don't know whether I would qualify?"

Counsellor: "Your reasons being, sort of...?"

Sue: "I'm not married and I don't want it."

Counsellor: "Yes. The doctor and the gynaecologist have to sign the form, you know, in good faith, but they obviously... the doctors and the gynics who work for an organisation that does terminations believe that this is a very necessary thing and they are very sympathetic and very understanding.

"And, usually, if you are on your own and feel that you can't cope with a child on your own, and you don't want to cope, and you don't want to have to try to support a child on your own, then they are very understanding like this.

"Usually, the main reasons why patients are refused is if they feel (the doctors) that there is any hesitancy. Perhaps they are being pushed into it by somebody else and really would rather go ahead if left to themselves and have the baby. Then none of the doctors will support this.

"And, obviously, of course, if they're too late. Say they are something like twenty weeks pregnant, well, it's very, very difficult to get a gynaecologist who will consider termination at that stage. But beyond those two cases, I don't think you will find any problem. I'll leave you with this card which tells you what the Pregnancy Advisory Service is and generally details. So, if you want to make an appointment?"

Sue: "Yes, I would like to. How soon do you think that I could go in?"

Counsellor: "They'll fit you in as soon as possible for an appointment, and you will see the doctor and the gynaecologist at the same time."

Sue: "The gynaecologist I see is the one who will do it, is he?"

Counsellor: "That's right, yes. He's a Harley Street specialist, so you'll be in good hands. You haven't anything to fear from that point of view. The gynaecologists are in Harley Street and Fitzroy Square, both of which are a couple of minutes from here, so you will go to one of them as soon as you've seen the counsellor and the doctor. You do all that in one go and then they make all the arrangements."

We did not keep any further appointments at the London PAS. Sue's interiew with the counsellor had revealed everything we wanted to discover about the rectitude or reverse of this establishment. Our conclusions are self-evident and require little appraisal or post-mortem.

. . . .

All doctors are entrusted, by the Act, to sanction abortions in "good faith". Yet every single doctor we encountered in the private sector, which includes those in the so-called "charitable" province, was acting perfidiously.

Under-cutting in the Abortion Supermarkets

Quite a high percentage of the doctors making fortunes for themselves in the British abortion industry are, to put it mildly, of dubious character and moral fragility. There are those who have been struck-off or suspended by their own medical bodies, either in Britain or other parts of the globe. Some have been working illegally while struck-off. Others, who have become re-instated after doing their penance, have found the abortion service the only sector of "medicine" prepared to give them employment. The truth is that private abortion is the slag-end of the medical profession. It attracts the profligates and the incompetent, because they are the only ones, in the main, who are prepared to stain their hands and souls in this sleazy surgery.

Most doctors enter their profession with the high and pure ideals of preserving life. Abortion, being the deliberate destruction of human life, therefore, is contrary and diametrically opposed to everything they cherish and hold dear. For them, it is politically, medically and morally abhorrent. But for some, corrosion sets in: some are struck-off, others fall short of their ambitions, while others turn Faust and sell out to the lure of wealth. Somewhere along the line, the majority of doctors in the private sector of abortion have compromised their ideals and their ethics.

One can understand the poor doctor, who is finding it difficult to obtain work, who, as a last and sorrowful resort, turns to abortion. One can understand the struck-off doctor, who, after being reinstated, sees abortion as the backdoor entrance in his bid for readmittance into "legitimate" medicine. One can understand them, without condoning them. One can condemn while appreciating the mitigating circumstances.

One has to be able to draw on great repositories of charity, though, to be able to forgive the gynaecologists who have prostituted themselves for money. The talented ones who could be zealously preserving life in accordance with their initial calling and who, instead, have become not passive but energetic participants of the killer syndrome, callously and calculatingly liquidating human life every day. These doctors, gynacologists, just kill every day of their lives. Many of them have done nothing in their profession other than kill every day for six years. Death has become part of their anatomy and instinct. There are gynaecologists who have forgotten what it is like to bring a baby *alive* into the world. All they ever see are dead babies, the ones they have killed, while their infant hearts were beating and their minds were functioning.

There is the additional danger here that we are breeding a killer mentality, men who see surgery as butchery. The mind boggles at the domestic scene when these doctors return to their families in the evening. Does the wife, in front of the children, say: "Have a good day at work today, darling?"

And the husband, smiling warmly, replies: "Not bad, darling, I burnt thirty babies to death. Average day. I've known better, though."

"Never mind, darling, perhaps you'll do better tomorrow," purrs the wife consolingly.

One of the doctors we investigated had been working for one of the "charitable" organisations after being struck-off for professional misconduct. He is Dr. Gilbert Dalley, who owned Fawkham Manor, a nursing home near Dartford, Kent, until selling it to the British Pregnancy Advisory Serice.

Now, it was the BPAS who employed Mr. Dalley when he was reinstated. The martinet protagonist of BPAS, the buxom and bellicose Mrs. Nan Smith, vehemently denies knowing Dr. Dalley had been struck off at the time she employed him at their clinic in Liverpool. Mrs. Smith claims that she learned of Dr. Dalley's record of professional misconduct only after he had left her organisation. He was not, of course, under suspension at the time he worked for her in Liverpool. However, after learning of his record, the BPAS decided to enter into a business transaction with him and buy his nursing home, Fawkham Manor. Following the purchase, BPAS applied for an abortion licence for Fawkham Manor, much to the horror and dismay of local residents.

Dr. Dalley was suspended in November, 1970, after being found guilty of "serious professional misconduct" for advertising abortion services to between seventy and eighty doctors in West Germany. He was also found guilty of falsely stating that his clinic was licensed to carry out abortions.

At the time of his suspension, he said: "At least patients who come to Fawkham Manor are received as human beings. If it wasn't for the abortions, I could not have kept open."

So BPAS have taken over a clinic where *illegal* abortions had been taking place. Mrs. Smith told us categorically that Dr. Dalley would have nothing whatsoever to do with the clinic now that it was owned by BPAS. When we contacted Dr. Dalley, he was living in a cottage directly opposite Fawkham Manor and he was often in the grounds, and we saw him, on numerous occasions, inspecting the workmanship of the builders who were doing renovations.

A newcomer at that time to the village in which Fawkham Manor is situated was Mr. Ronald Shaw. Now Mr. Shaw owns the abortion clinic, the London Private Nursing Home, Langham Street, London, to which Sue was referred for an operation after the interview with Mrs. Sue Maxwell, of the pregnancy advisory service in Lancashire Court, also owned by Mr. Shaw.

Mr. Shaw has a varied range of business interests in addition to abortion, including garages, population control project companies, and agencies for managing 'Pop' stars, theatrical artistes and writers. When we asked Mrs. Nan Smith if there was any connection between her organisation and Mr. Shaw, she said: "No, there is not. He did make an approach to me at one stage, but I said that I did not see any possibility of our two organisations getting together in any way."

So Mr. Shaw's domestic move to within a few hundred yards of Fawkham Manor was purely coincidental, we asked her: "Quite so," she replied. "He did, however, ask if he could help with providing workmen because he knew we were having trouble with the builders. Workmen are always our biggest headache..."

The nursing home owned by Mr. Shaw was the notorious Langham Street Clinic, which was closed down under the previous ownership. Mr. Shaw bought the clinic and it was given a new licence. He also changed its name to the London Private Nursing Home Ltd., though it retained the same telephone number as when it was the Langham Clinic, and many of the same doctors continued to work there.

When we approached Dr. Dalley, we did so under the guise of business people trying to infiltrate the abortion industry in Britain. The following dialogue is a tape-recorded conversation between Dr. Dalley and Litchfield:

Litchfield: "I suppose it's very much better to take over an existing building than starting from scratch?"

Dr. Dalley: "Well, there are all sorts of aspects to this. You see, BPAS, in respect of Fawkham Manor, haven't yet got planning permission."

Litchfield: "I was under the impression that they had?"

Dr. Dalley: "I don't think they have. There's been a certain amount of local opposition. I'm almost sure they haven't got a licence yet. I think, possibly, they will get one. That, I think, is the current position."

Litchfield: "Would the Midlands or North be better, do you suppose, than the South of England for starting an abortion clinic?"

Dr. Dalley: "I think it possibly would be, although I don't have a lot of first-hand experience of those areas. The point is that they have large centres of population and some of them, at least, have, possibly, almost more money available than London. I mean *patient money*, that is.

"London scores by being the capital and also attracting foreign customers, whereas other areas have to depend on the local catchment area. The climate, as regards granting of licences, is much more lenient now than it was. In fact, some might say it had almost gone too far. Like hotels, there's almost a surplus of beds."

Litchfield: "So it could be cut-throat down in the south?"

Dr. Dalley: "Well, it is. There are one or two big organisations that can afford to under-cut some of the others. There is an amount of price-cutting going on."

This is really demoting human life to supermarket leel: babies' lives on special offer "trading stamps and a free gift for giving us the concession rights on murdering your child..."

"It's been going on for the past six months," Dr. Dalley claimed. "I think it would be dicey to open a place at the moment I don't think the market is likely to get better. It's running fairly steady at about 200,000 to 300,000 a year."

This is much more than the official Government figure, but it is likely to be the more precise one. It is well-known that income tax avoidance is one of the major corruptions of the abortion industry. Thousands upon thousands of the official green abortion forms are destroyed, instead of being returned completed to the Ministry of Health, so the actual number of yearly abortions in Britain is pure speculation. The forms relating to abortions on foreign girls are the most abused, because it is in this area that the clinics are least likely to be exposed.

"The question is whether there are not already enough beds to cope with that." he said. "And with this price-cutting going on..."

Litchfield: "Is there scope for an expensive clinic?"

Dr. Dalley: "This is the funny thing, they all prefer to get it the cheapest way possible."

Litchfield: "Is it better for businessmen to keep in the background and have somebody from the medical world as a 'front'?"

Dr. Dalley: "My feeling is that rather the reverse has been the case here. As far as history goes, they have preferred, well, this is the inference, that they preferred to grant licenses to non-medical people. Obviously, one has to employ doctors to do the work. But they seem to prefer that the organisers should be non-medical.

"As far as I'm concerned, Fawkham Manor is sold. They are still doing the alterations, but, as I say, they haven't yet got a licence. I wouldn't have thought that they would have had much trouble getting it, but they are not entirely going the easiest way about it. They are tending to do things without asking planning permission first. Also, they've been very high-handed with almost everybody.

"They seem to think that they have a divine right and everybody must automatically follow their line. They have this expansion attitude. It's run by this woman, Mrs. Nan Smith, with headquarters in Birmingham. They also have places in Brighton, Leamington Spa and Liverpool."

Litchfield: "They must be making it pay?"

Dr. Dalley: "Oh, they do."

Litchfield: "But are they doing it on the cheap?"

Dr. Dalley: "As far as doctors are concerned. But not on the administrative or clerical side. Yes, they are undercutting."

"Also, you see, they have been very clever and registered themselves as a charity and they don't pay tax (he laughed). They are doing very, very well. Mrs. Smith is full-time in the business. She is not a doctor. She's a woman who likes to project herself as someone with a mission. She really likes to be boss woman.

"She's quite approachable. She'd see you definitely as opposition, though. I mean, she'd probably offer to buy you out, or something like that. She'd say, 'you come in opposition and we'll undercut you and then we'll take over your place...'

"She thinks that she's on the right side of certain people in high places, so that anybody else can go and stuff themselves."

Several doctors we spoke to, talked of money that clinics were paying in 'backhanders'. These bribes were costed as part of the abortion overheads, as has been the case for so long in the building industry, in which tenders to certain local authorities have to include the bribe to officials. This is nothing new in the building industry. It has been accepted for a long, long time by people in the trade. The abortionists are beginning to talk more openly themselves now about the graft in their line of business. It should not, of course, come as any surprise. Where there's muck, there is always dirt money. None of the doctors who disclosed facts about bribery worked for BPAS, incidentally.

When we asked Mrs. Smith if she would like to talk to us about our findings regarding BPAS, she told us (again it was tape-recorded): "We are a charitable trust. I would have thought we were as proud as we can be of our organisation. Of course we're proud of the work we do.

"We don't make profits from the work we do, and none of the people who work for us make a profit." This is bending the truth. A great deal of money goes into the pockets of the doctors and the staff.

"If anything goes wrong in any of the branches of my organisation, I am prepared to take the responsibility."

Referring to Dr. Dalley, whom she employed after he had been struck-off, she said: "All I knew about him was that he was a gentleman who applied to us for work. We gave him work. He applied to us as a surgeon some time back. He worked at one of our nursing homes, at Liverpool, for a short period. In fact, it was subsequent to his ceasing to work for us that we learned about him."

"Will he ever work for you again?" she was asked.

"He won't now, though he did at one time," she said.

We then turned to the topic of Mr. Shaw, owner of the money-spinning Langham Clinic, which is very much to the fore of the private and pricey abortion zone.

"The name rings a bell," she mused. "I can't think where I know the name from, but I do know it..."

Litchfield prodded her memory.

"Oh, I've just remembered who Mr. Shaw is!" she exclaimed suddenly. "Mr. Shaw is the man who runs the Langham Clinic. I know nothing about the man at all. I have been to the Langham Clinic. I was offered it for sale. I looked at it and decided it wasn't suitable for our purposes. We turned it down as being completely unsuitable for us. We have far better clinics than that.

"Mr. Shaw telephoned on one occasion to ask if we could get together. And I said that there was no possibility of our organisation having any connection with his. That's all I know about the man. He said that we were having great difficulty with our builders at Fawkham Manor. We were. He wanted to help us as he was living near by. And that is all I know about him. I didn't want anything to do with his organisation because his isn't a charity in the way that we are."

Section 4: **Babies for the Soap Factory**

Babies for the Soap Factory

We were sitting in yet another dowdy doctor's surgery in Harley Street. The doctor, one of the tawdry speculators in the private goldmining industry, otherwise known as abortion, was reeling off one excuse after another for his "unwitting involvement" in a trade which, in his own words, had "sold its soul for silver". He was caught on the treadmill... fastened to the wheel... ensnared by his unscrupulous and vicious colleagues... a victim of circumstance... a casualty of a sick society... Name an excuse, and he thought of it.

He started to cry. You might be surprised at the number of doctors responsible for killing thousands of defenceless babies every year in cold blood, who, when confronted with their heinous crimes, wept in the manner their little victims will never weep...

This particular loathsome doctor buried his head in his hands and pleaded with us: "I have a family... we are all flouting the law, but some are worse than others... I'm not one of Harley Street's real gangsters... there are many, but I'm not one... if you spare me, I'll tell you about a real villain, can we do a deal? (They're very good at doing deals.) Show me charity and I'll never do another abortion in my life... I know it's wrong and wicked, we all do really, but no one will take a stand and say, 'enough' and stop... what about a deal?"

We said that we could not make any promises, but we invited him to confide in us about the "real gangster" and allow us in "good faith", which he ought to know all about considering that phrase is the legendary, infamous loophole in the Abortion Act, to use our discretion. Rightly or wrongly, we showed the kind of compassion of which he knows nothing, and we do not publicly declare his name, though it has been submitted to the appropriate authorities.

"There's one gynaecologist, here in Harley Street, not far from me, who... you will find this hard to believe because it's so revolting... well, he sells the foetuses to a factory... a chemical factory... they make soap and cosmetics... and they... er... pay very well, indeed, for babies because animal fat is very precious, gold dust in their line..." he stammered nervously.

We had reached the stage when we believed there was nothing left to shock us in the British abortion panorama. We were wrong. Each time we thought that we had become numb and seasoned to the nausea, so a new and more sickening experience seized and reawakened our revulsion and rekindled our shame at being members of a society that had licensed all this degradation, human contamination and pollution.

This doctor volunteered the identity of the gynaecologist involved in selling babies to soap manufacturers. It was obvious that the gynaecologist would not openly admit to his gruesome and sub-human, sub-animal activities. So we debated, and agreed to approach him as a rival manufacturer and make a counter-bid for the foetuses. This we did. Firstly, we telephoned him. His secretary told Litchfield that he was at the clinic operating.

Litchfield immediately contacted the clinic and spoke to another of the gynaecologist's secretaries there. "Can you tell me something about the matter?" she asked.

"Yes," said Litchfield, "I am interested in buying foetuses from Mr... I understand he is selling them to a factory in the East End of London at the moment. I am prepared to bid above them. I represent a rival firm..."

"Well," said the secretary, "I don't know about that... er... I'm not sure... I think you had better talk to Mr... about that. It's not something I can discuss, really, because it's a matter only he could deal with. I believe, actually, it is illegal to sell the foetus, but I would rather not know anything about that side of his business, if you see what I mean. Can I get him to telephone you when he comes out of the theatre?"

"No, I'll call him back."

"Can I say who rang?"

A name was given, but we declined to state a company. It seemed better to create an air of mystery and intrigue, that was bound to bite at the gynaecologist's curiosity... and greed.

The same afternoon, Litchfield again telephoned the clinic. Mr... was available this time. "Yes, I received the message," he said. "Now, this is a tricky matter. I don't think it wise to talk over the telephone. How did you learn about me?"

"A contact," Litchfield said obliquely.

"I see... I see... It's delicate, you know, we have to be very careful. The best thing is for you to come and see me in Harley Street. Ring my secretary in Harley Street and make an appointment for tomorrow morning. Then we can discuss the whole thing in private."

A meeting was arranged for 11 a.m. the following day at his surgery in Harley Street.

When we met, the gynaecologist asked his secretary to leave the room, leaving himself and Litchfield alone in his sumptuous office, which exhibited all the trappings of opulence. He came and perched himself on the edge of his massive, oak desk, which was very considerate of him because it meant he was speaking almost directly into the microphone of our tape-recorder, which was hidden in a leather briefcase.

He waved a letter in front of Litchfield's face. "This is from the Ministry of Health," he said, twisting his face in a display of disgust. "They say here, you see, that we have to burn the foetuses... that we mustn't sell them for anything, not even research... you see, it's a problem..."

"But you already sell your foetuses to a cosmetics factory..." reminded Litchfield.

"You say so... I'm not saying 'yes' and I'm not saying 'no'... You see, I want to co-operate, but it's difficult. We have to consider the law.

"Local residents in the vicinity of my clinic have been complaining about the smell of burning flesh. The smell comes from the incinerator. It does make a stink. They say

147

it smells like a Nazi extermination camp during the last War. I don't know how they would know what the German camps smelt like, but I do not dispute the fact. So I am always looking for ways of disposing of the foetuses, other than burning them.

"You see, there isn't much money in flogging them for research. It's all a question of what is worth my while... and how they can be taken away without my breaking the law..."

"Well, how do you arrange it with the firm you deal with in the East End of London?"

"Ah, well, now... you see... I would not have to know officially what is going on... the foetuses, as far as I'm aware, are prepared for the incinerator, then they disappear. I don't know what happens to them. They just vanish. You have to make all arrangements for a van or lorry or something to come to the rear entrance. Times and so forth would have to be arranged later. This all depends, of course, on our coming to some form of agreement. There is, of course, the financial... you know... what are you prepared to offer?"

"What are you getting at the moment?"

"You see, I get some very big babies. It's such a shame to toss them in the incinerator, when they could be put to so much better use. We do a lot of late terminations. We specialise in them. I do ones that other people won't touch. I do them at seven months without hesitation. The law says twenty-eight weeks is the legal limit, but it is impossible to determine at what stage a termination was performed after the baby is burned, so it does not matter when one does it, really. If the mother is prepared to take the risk, then I'm game.

"Now, many of the babies I get are fully-formed and are living for quite a time before they are disposed of. One morning, I had four of them lined up crying their heads off. I hadn't the time to kill them there and then because we were so busy. I was so loathe to drop them in the incinerator because there was so much animal fat that could have been used commercially.

"They could live at that stage if they were put in an

incubator, but we don't have those kind of facilities in my clinic. Our business is ending lives, not helping to get them started.

"I'm not a hard man, just realistic. If I'm paid to do a job, that's getting rid of a baby, then it would be a breach of contract if I allowed that child to live, even though I may keep it alive for half an hour, or so. I have some trouble with the nursing staff. Many of them faint on their first day. We have a terrible turnover of staff. The Germans are often very good. They are not all that squeamish as a race. The English can be a bit too sentimental, but not always.

"Hitler may have been the enemy of this country, but not everything about his policies was bad. He had some very progressive ideas and philosophies. Selective life has always appealed to certain elements of the medical world. I've always been drawn to the possibility of selective breeding and selective elimination. But that's another matter... I'm sorry to bore you with my theories. I bet you think I'm a bit mad? If I am, then I'm not alone. Many, many gynaecologists doing terminations in London and elsewhere in Britain think the same way as I do. But you have to be a man of science and not of emotion, to see through the fog of sentimentality. Human life is just a matter that can be controlled, conditioned and defused like any machine.

"Now, you are not a biochemist, are you?"

"No," Litchfield replied.

"A pity. I would like to meet your biochemist. You see, you say that you want the foetuses for cosmetic soap, but there is a much more valuable use to which they can be applied."

"What else can they be used for?"

"It's no good talking to anyone who is not a biochemist. But there is a very special... very profitable... it could be to our mutual benefit."

"I'll get our biochemist to contact you," Litchfield promised.

"Yes, please do that. Then we can draw up some kind of contract. It will probably have to be a sort of *gentleman's agreement.* That's how I've got it arranged with the other firm. Now, not a word with anyone, please. We have to be very, very discreet. Then we can talk money. And we shall benefit from each other. Perhaps we shall become friends? I hope so."

There was no suitable reply to that, other than to leave as speedily as possible. We did not return with a biochemist. We had uncovered sufficient about the subterfuge and corruption of this "man".

Later, when we spoke to this grotesque gynaecologist, telling him of our research and our authentic identity, he retorted: "Please do not blame the gynaecologists for what is happening in this country. We are not to blame. It has been forced on us. If we don't do it, someone else will.

"We are the end of the line. The girls are pushed on to us by all these other people and we cannot turn our backs on these women. As a profession, we have prostituted ourselves. It would not have happened if we had a trade union. Then, the union would say, 'no abortions', and anyone breaking that ruling would be a 'blackleg' and struck off. As it is, it is just a free-for-all, everything goes, and we just go from bad to worse.

"I wish somebody would stop us. I would love to be able to buy back my conscience..."

Section 5: **Abortion and After**

The Daily Agony

To wake every day knowing you have killed another human being is the daily hell that faces every person involved in the network of abortion sewers.

To wake every day, when the sun shines, the rain falls, knowing that YOUR OWN child will never tumble into your bedroom to shake you awake, tripping out childish demands, will never experience even the most trite of human emotions — is an agony beyond the conception of anyone who has not had an abortion.

This irreparable remorse was described to us by Yvonne, a 23-year-old office worker from the Midlands of England, who had an abortion nearly five years ago, in November 1969. To all intents and purposes, she is a normal newly-wed, proud of the possessions she and her husband have collected together and keen to move to a more select area of the city, where she can leave outside her front door one of those nice white plastic milk crates with dials, without fear of it being stolen.

Behind her long, dark hair and almost black eyes are many signs of her daily agony, easy to distinguish because they fall into a pattern to be found in women who have had an abortion: she is on tranquillisers... some days she plays rapturously with her brother's two young daughters, other days she inwardly hates them...she cries off social events at the very last moment, just as she and her husband are stepping across the door mat... and in recent months, she has found herself unable to face shopping alone in the city centre or a simple trip, such as going to the dentist... and since her marriage she has had a burning conviction that she is sterile...

Let Yvonne tell her own story:

"I was 18 and my boyfriend and I had been sleeping

together. This one night I did something I had never done before, I stayed out all night, telling my father I would be sleeping at a girlfriend's. It was the first time he hadn't taken precautions and the next morning, standing in the bathroom, I knew I was pregnant. I can't tell you how, I just felt odd.

"For the next five months I told myself constantly that I wasn't pregnant. I dreamt up all sorts of excuses. I simply couldn't face up to it. I was terribly sick in the mornings and I would go into the bathroom and turn on the sink taps full so that my father wouldn't hear.

"I got terribly tired. I would nod off on buses, get home and go to bed at six and still be tired the following morning. Even then, I didn't tell. My father had so much on his plate already. Mum had left home a few months previously; her nerves were bad.

"In the end, I walked into the big store where my brother was working at the time, collapsed and told him. He said we had to tell Dad at once and took me home.

"Dad's immediate reaction was to get an abortion, nobody thought of anything else. He contacted Mum and she came home — it's awful to think it brought about their reconciliation — and within a week, I had had the abortion. I was swept along, there was no time to think and nobody made me or my parents stop and think. Nobody suggested alternatives or talked about adoption.

"It was all, how it would ruin my life... I was so young... the boyfriend wasn't a suitable husband... no man would want an unmarried mum... what the neighbours would say. They were right about one thing, the boyfriend. I believed myself to be in love with him, but really he didn't want to know and he only came to see me twice after it was all over. He was never in work and he wouldn't have been a good husband for me.

"Well, my Dad took me to the family doctor who said I was about four-and-a-half to five months. He said he was against abortion, and in any case, it was far too late. He said he didn't want to know if I was going to have an abortion, but if I did to tell him afterwards — for my medical records! He advised us to get in touch with the Pregnancy

Advisory Service in Birmingham (now the British Pregnancy Advisory Service).

"My Dad phoned them up, it was nearly all arranged on the telephone, and I had to go and see a woman, who described herself as a social worker, at her home in a back street. She asked very few questions and one of the first was, 'It'll be £150 — can you afford it?' She said, if not, arrangements could possibly be made for something cheaper. She charged £8, which she waffled about and tried to explain that it was passed on to the doctor. Advice service. The only advice they gave me was how to go about getting an abortion. What I needed was advice about how it was a baby, a living human being and what best I could do for it.

"Do you know that at no time did anyone talk of the baby as a baby. They all try to make you believe it's nothing, something to be got rid of as quickly as possible. These people were wicked, all they wanted was my money, they didn't care about me or my baby inside me.

"This woman at PAS sent me to Dr. Sisar Dutta in Birmingham, who told me to go to the Lady Margaret Nursing Home in Ealing, London, the following Sunday, with the money in cash in a white envelope. He said he would do the abortion. He didn't examine me then or at any time.

"My father didn't have the money right off. He went to the bank manager who was a friend of his and asked for a loan. The manager asked what it was for and my father said it was personal. The manager said he had to know what the money was going to be used for with a personal loan.

"My father said; 'My daughter's in trouble,' and the manager replied: 'Oh, you want it for an abortion, that's all right.'

"That whole week was dogged by a catalogue of people any one of whom might have said something to make us stop and think, but none of them did. It was so horribly easy to fix up.

"On the Saturday evening, the woman from PAS rang up and persistently offered me a lift to the clinic on a coach — for an extra £5. She said the coach would pick me up and deliver me and the other girls to the clinic and drop us all back at our doorsteps.

"But I went with my brother and boyfriend. My brother said he didn't approve of abortions, but he wouldn't go against Dad, and my boyfriend just tagged along.

"When I arrived at the clinic, I was shown into a ward with about twenty other girls. I was told to sit on the bed and wait for the nurse to collect the envelopes. She came round and counted out the contents of each one. Then I was told to get undressed and escorted upstairs three flights to the operating theatre. My blood was not checked. I was asked no questions. The last thing I remember is the anaesthetist telling me to lie down on the operating table, seeing Doctor Dutta who had on his operating gown and mask, and then the injection.

"I regained consciousness to see several doctors sitting around a table eating their dinner. They were in operating theatre gowns, their masks were around their necks and they still had on Wellington boots.

"I was in great pain, a nurse helped me off the table and I was made to walk down the three flights of stairs to my bed. I had to stop on the landings because of the pain. I collapsed on to the bed, I was bleeding heavily. I thought something must be wrong because I was the first to go up to the operating theatre and the last to come down. All the other girls were walking around, none appeared to be in pain. A nurse made me get up. 'Walk around,' she said, 'you'll feel a lot better, you won't help yourself lying around.' I noticed that mine was the only bed covered in blood. When I complained of the pain she told me, 'it's natural afterwards.'

"My brother came for me and was terribly worried. We waited ages to see somebody in charge about the bleeding and the pain, and finally my brother said he thought he had better get me home.

"I was in a state of collapse. I could hardly walk, all my clothes underneath my coat were seeped in blood. The clinic people just wanted to get rid of me, nobody asked me how I was, and I didn't even see Dr. Dutta after the operation. I wasn't even given tablets to take away the milk from my breasts.

"When we arrived at my home station, I couldn't move. I collapsed on to my suitcase and my brother had to phone my parents who came to collect me. I thought I was dying.

"My mother put me to bed and for three days I was in agony with labour pains. The woman at PAS told my mother when she telephoned, 'Don't worry, give her some painkillers.' The pain got worse, not better and finally she called the doctor. He laid his hands on my stomach and said: 'You haven't had an abortion, you're still pregnant.' An ambulance was called and I was taken to hospital. Whilst I was lying in casualty a white 'lump' was taken away from me. I was told that the abortion had been incomplete, that I had been stitched up and that part of the baby had been left inside me.

"I was in hospital for a month, the first week I had six injections a day and then the placenta came away. I was told if it had stayed inside me any longer I would certainly have been sterile. All the time I was in there, I thought I was dying. My father blamed himself, he couldn't bear to face me, he was too ashamed to visit me in hospital.

"I was in a bad state mentally when I got home and for a long time afterwards. It had all seemed such a problem when I had been pregnant. I was only 18 and at that age you don't think of all the aspects, you just want it to go away. But I didn't want to kill it. Despite my horror at being pregnant, one part of my mind had delighted in the morning sickness and the baby kicking, like butterflies fluttering inside. Then there was nothing. I wondered whether it had been a boy or a girl, what colour its hair was. I would lie on my bed at home and dream that it had never happened, that I had a living baby, that it was gurgling happily in the next room.

"I would pretend about my baby, that it was living and then I would wake up to the horrible truth. I had all sorts of fantasies. I looked at babies in prams. And I went to Mothercare where I would finger the baby clothes and pretend. But I never did buy anything.

"Eventually I started going out again socially, but I spurned men. I led them on and then wouldn't let them so much as kiss me on the cheek, I hated all men.

"I'm sure if I hadn't met my future husband last year I would have gone mad. As it was, I was enormously rude to him whenever he tried to talk to me, but he persisted and after the first date, that was that. Two months later, we were engaged. When I told my parents they said I ought to tell him about the abortion. He said it didn't make any difference and that he still loved me and wanted to marry me.

"For a while things were fine, planning the wedding and our home and I felt happy. But since our marriage, I have become terribly depressed. I'm on tranquillisers and I find it increasingly difficult to go out alone during the daytime or even socially with my husband. He has to come everywhere with me, even to do the shopping. I still have nightmares about it all, and I know that even if there had not been all the grisly circumstances surrounding my abortion, mentally and emotionally the effect would be the same.

"We wanted to have children right from the beginning and though we have never used contraceptives, I have still not conceived. I had worked myself up into a real state and was convinced until a week ago that I was sterile. I was warned in the hospital that this was a possibility, but I hadn't thought about it since, until my marriage. I know it's silly, but I felt this was a retribution. But I've been examined and had tests, and I'm told there's nothing wrong, except for my nerves and the state of my mind.

"I've got babies on my mind all the time. Every morning after we've made love I wonder whether I'm pregnant. I can't do anything without babies cropping up. Have you noticed how all the television adverts use babies?

"My period is two days overdue now and I'm keeping my fingers crossed. But it's nothing to go by, my periods have never been right since the abortion. We've got the baby's room all ready, just in case. I'm just so desperate to be pregnant, to create life. If only somebody had pointed out that the baby I was carrying was a life, that it might be the wrong time but that I didn't have the right to kill it. All I needed was sympathy and advice. Is that too much to ask?

"Yet look what's happened, abortion is on demand more than ever now. That Dr. Dutta faced an inquiry over my case, but he wasn't struck-off until some time later when he was found guilty of advertising! And the clinic was closed only after a woman had died there.

"Do you know, I met a young girl in there who was only 15, and she had come with her boyfriend, her parents didn't even know. Goodness knows where they got the money. Supposing she had had the same repercussions as me, she could have gone back to her flat and died without anyone knowing.

"Girls really don't know what they're doing, it's all so easy. Two girls at work started talking about having children. They were both newly married, with big mortgages and on the Pill, and neither planned to have children for several years. I asked one what she would do if she accidentally got pregnant and she said it just wouldn't happen, and the other girl said to her: 'But suppose it did happen, what would you do?' And she replied: 'I'd get an abortion, I know where you can go for one.'

"I said, but hadn't she thought what she would be doing, the emotional reaction that would follow? She said: 'Nonsense, it's done all the time, I wouldn't care.'

"Then I said that it was wrong and that it was murder, and she said; 'Well, you read about it all the time in the papers. Of course it's not murder.'

"You see, no one who has not had an abortion can really appreciate what it is like. The young girl who walks out of one of those places may feel that it was nothing.

"It may not hit her immediately or in the days that follow: the effects may come years later, but be sure, they will come. There is no escape from the remorse and realisation that abortion is murder.

"With me, the effects have come in waves, always there, sometimes just quietly lapping at my mind, at others almost engulfing me.

"It is something you can never forget and the guilty weight on your mind never goes away."

. . . .

It seemed a good idea at the time. In so much as she thought about it at all. She loved the man, lived with him and cared for his young daughter. So she stopped taking the Pill. After all, with the reported side effects — blood-clotting five times more common — it seemed an unnecessary risk.

The effects have been cataclysmic for Nancy, her lover and his child by a previous marriage. In the last year their separate and united worlds have been thrown upside down.

Let Nancy tell her story:

"I suppose you could say it all started when I went for the job. I'd always been a nanny you see. I love kids, and I've got a large family at home, and this was a local job. I was a bit startled when I saw my prospective boss — well, he was so young and good-looking, too. Not that I took much notice of that. But he seemed kind and I liked the little girl. He needed a mother for his daughter, somebody to live in, do a bit of cooking and generally care for Jane who had just started school. It wasn't a posh home like I'd been used to and you could tell he hadn't taken much interest in the house since his wife had left.

"Looking back, I suppose you could see the signs: I mean, there was this broken home, just needing a woman and there was I, 18 and single and unattached. First it started with little things, like I tried to make the house more homely, more lived in. I did more than the job called for, but I was happy.

"It was nicer than other jobs I had had, because Gregory and Jane made me feel part of the family; they wouldn't let me remain alone all evening in my bedroom, they invited me to join them downstairs. And after I had put Jane to bed, I would stay on downstairs, watching telly. Gradually, our relationship changed. He stopped going out with his friends so much at night-time, preferring to stay with me. Well, pretty soon our relationship developed from friendship to love.

"I can't really say why I stopped taking the Pill. It wasn't a terribly conscious thing, I mean, I didn't say out loud, 'I'm not going to take the Pill any more, I want to become pregnant.' I just stopped. One night I didn't bother, then the next and the next.

"Of course, the inevitable happened, I became pregnant, but for some reason I can't explain, I didn't say anything. Finally, at three months, I told Greg I thought I was pregnant. He packed me off to the doctor for confirmation and that's when the panic set in. You see, he never said he would marry me, but I'd always assumed that once he was divorced he would do so. So, when he told me he intended never to marry again, I was shattered. I was numb, frozen, my limbs dragged my mind along. He wasn't chucking me out, just refusing to marry me. Said it was my decision whether to go on with the baby or have an abortion. Suddenly, there was this terrible gulf. I was on my own. As far as I was able to think at all, I knew then, when I found I couldn't understand him any longer, that we didn't have a stable relationship. I could have screamed aloud with the agony of the loneliness of it all. He refused to participate in the decision — but said he would stand by me whatever!

"I couldn't understand, I just couldn't understand. 'He doesn't love me, he doesn't love me,' I told myself repeatedly. Surely, if he had, he would have wrapped me in his arms and said how marvellous it all was. Instead, he was trying to do the 'right thing' by standing by me, even though he didn't love me and — by implication — didn't want my child.

"So I got an abortion. My God, it was all so easy. I mean, you want an abortion — so you look in the small ads in the paper or the yellow pages of the telephone directory for pregnancy testing. Would you believe, some even advertise abortions as part of their service! I went to a place in London and two days later it was all fixed up — for around £75. Greg got the money, came with me to the hospital and picked me up the following day. I can't say there was a lot to it, because there wasn't. It was like going into hospital for a minor operation. After the anaesthetic, I didn't feel a thing, and the next I knew was waking up feeling drowsy. All I recall clearly is my panic because I had no sanitary towels and I didn't like to ask the nurses for a fresh one. They had warned me at the pregnancy advisory place that the abortion would bring on my period and instructed me to bring some STs, but I just forgot.

"When Greg collected me he was all cheerful and smiling. I felt okay, but drained somehow. When we got home, nothing had changed, the house was the same, little Jane was pleased to see me, but I felt depressed. It was from that moment, I suppose, that I began feeling hate. He expected me to carry on as if nothing had happened.

"For the first time, the impact of it all hit me. I mean, it was a very important thing that I had done, and yet here he was treating it as unimportant. And then there was Jane, wanting this, wanting that, asking this, asking that. I couldn't stand it. I argued with Greg and yelled at Jane.

"Of course, I got over the depression in time. But I changed, I know I did. 'Right,' I thought, 'He's been selfish, so that's how I'll be from now on.' If he still wanted me — and he said he did — then he would have to accept me on my terms. First, a new home. Because this one, despite what I had done to it, was his wife's. Second, he had to choose between me and the child, the product of that marriage that had turned him off marrying again for life. I felt I was being logical. He regretted having married the first time because of the pain it had brought him, so he must rid himself of everything connected with that marriage. It tore him in two.

"He told me the child came first, so I left. Within days, he begged me to return. I agreed on the understanding that Jane was NOT part of the bargain — he must get a new nanny for her, because I certainly wasn't going to have anything to do with her. I triumphed. He agreed, pleading with me to return. I got a job during the day so he was forced to find somebody else to look after Jane and collect her from school and in the evenings he packed her off to bed early. At weekends, she was sent to her grandparents.

"Then I got pregnant again, less than three months after the abortion.

"It was a pure accident. I mean, I was on the coil at the time. I couldn't believe it, I just couldn't believe it could happen to me again so soon. And would you credit it? — Despite all that had happened before and the fact that he loved me and said he wanted me always by him, his attitude was precisely the same as before: the decision was mine.

"But this time he didn't bother to discuss with me the pros and cons. He said if he persuaded me to keep it and then our relationship went wrong in the future, I would throw reprisals at him for lumbering me with the child; and alternatively, if he persuaded me to have an abortion, I would later regret it and blame him. So he reckoned that if he took a back seat and remained impartial — impartial! Well, I ask you! — then I wouldn't blame him either way.

"Of course I blame him. I blame him for being fifty percent responsible for creating the child, and then refusing to take on fifty percent of the responsibility for deciding what to do about it.

"I felt sick in my heart. I believe that part of me will always hate him and Jane, the child he not only allowed to be born but welcomed. I hate his so-called liberality which to me is indifference. And what makes me scream inside is that we both love children. His idea of a happy life is a nine-to-five job that doesn't demand too much and gives him a reasonable standard of living and a woman at home, and lots of children. How I hate that word children. You ought to see him with Jane, and other children, he's great with them.

"So I got a second abortion.

"I couldn't go back to the same place so soon. So I went to another, virtually around the corner. It was easier there. I was prepared to say I had never been pregnant nor had an abortion. As it was, nobody asked. Getting the abortion was even simpler. Like the first time, I just said I wasn't married and there was no opportunity of marrying the father and that was that. This one was even cheaper, it cost £50. This time I remembered the sanitary towels...

"You can't go back. I only wish you could. Just twelve months, that's all I want to relive, the last twelve months. How can I put it? It's like a long tunnel, I was at one end and pregnant. Looking through, I could see light at the other end, a dull grim light of an uncertain future, certainly not the right time for a child to be born, the problems ruled out going on with either child. Now I'm at the other end of that tunnel, and so I can see further to things that were previously beyond the horizon. I can see what happens if you have an abortion. I can see that I've rejected his child and got rid of two of my own. However unstable our relationship was then, it doesn't compare with the instability now. I mean, how can aborting two children who were the result of our love for each other provide a firm foundation for our future? He loves me still and that makes it even worse, because it shows me that there was no need to have an abortion on the grounds of instability.

"I know I'm talking round in circles. Does all this make sense to you? And then there's Jane, who thankfully is going off to boarding school soon, so I won't be constantly reminded of what I might have had.

"That's the trouble you see, you don't think far enough ahead, you don't realise you can't turn back the clock and bring back the children as easily as you got rid of them.

"If you have had anybody close to you die then you'll know what I mean when I say it's like that — regretting, too late, the things you didn't do or in my case, the things you did do, and knowing, however much you may wish, that it's too late. Funny, I think of my childhood a lot these days and one of the things I vividly remember is the pain of learning that you can't stop the clock, of lying in bed on Boxing Day night and crying my heart out because the good time of Christmas was over. Why, why does that picture come to me now? Why couldn't it come a year ago?

"As for the future, I've no idea what will happen to us, we're drifting on, I don't want to leave him, but I'm not really happy with him. I wonder how much my children would have been like Jane, would they have been cleverer, prettier, or boys perhaps? I know he would have loved a son. It all seems so senseless now I'm older and wiser. I built mountains out of the molehill-size problems and made the mountains, the babies themselves, out to be molehills. And I overlooked Jane, I didn't realise I would reject her. She needs love so much, too, more so than other children because of the broken marriage, and I can't give it to her. I'm glad she's going to boarding school. She's eight, which is perhaps a bit young, but she'll soon grow and she seems to like the prospect. It will relieve the tension between Greg and me. It seems a good idea."

. . . .

Trim and slim in her pretty blue trouser suit, Janice walked down the path away from the clinic, vanity bag dangling from one hand and sunglasses from the other. She turned the corner and purposefully moved up the road. Then she saw it, standing back, set apart, the notice discreet but clear: "Home for Unmarried Mothers". She paced up and down outside with the appearance of waiting for someone. She looked over the hedge. Disappointment. No one there. A pram, she could see a pram in the covered entrance. Should she look? There was no one around. Hastily she pushed open the gate and walked up the path. She held her breath and leant over the navy blue hood. Her heart sunk. It was empty. Slowly, not caring now if she was spotted, she retraced her steps. Her reverie was broken by human noises. She looked up. Negotiating the kerb were two mothers with prams. Alongside a third young girl in a drab dress. Pregnant. Fat. Bursting. And smiling. Indecent. Nausea rose to her throat. Horrid cow. She ran...

"It all seems such a long time ago now, another world. It's been two years. April 21st., actually," Janice recalled when we spoke to her at her home in Yorkshire. "I ran away from the unmarried home as if the devil was at my heels. At length, exhausted, I returned to the clinic where my husband was waiting having arrived just after I left. Daft. I've no idea what made me go up to the unmarried home. Somebody had mentioned in the clinic that it was there and I had this passionate urge to see a real live baby.

"I'd had my abortion the previous afternoon and felt nothing about it until the following morning when from the moment of awakening, I felt I wanted to see a baby.

"It's perhaps difficult for you to understand but until the day after the operation I hadn't thought of 'it' as a baby. When I had found my husband and I had slipped up and I was pregnant, the answer was obvious. Abortion. I had always thought that if I became pregnant at the wrong time this would be the ideal solution. We had been married only a few months, we were still building up our home, paying off a hefty mortgage and we had no carpets. Besides we wanted a few years together before starting a family. I went to a pregnancy advisory establishment in Birmingham and they fixed it for me. It was surprisingly quick, a week to the day of the confirmation of pregnancy. There was a lot of paperwork involved at the clinic, a lot of questions about our sex lives and background. Nobody questioned my decision to have an abortion, I merely said I didn't want to go on with it, that I wasn't ready for a child. The following week I presented myself and the money — about £70 in cash, I think — at the clinic and that was that.

"My husband and I didn't discuss the abortion much, we talked mainly about how we hoped the operation was safe. And as I say, it didn't strike me till the day after that what I had got rid of was not an 'it', not a lump of jelly but 'my baby'. When it wasn't there any more, when it had gone, it then, and only then, became real.

"When I met my husband back at the clinic, I just said I'd been out for a walk to stretch my legs. We got home and another overwhelming urge struck me — to touch a baby, to stroke its face, feel its soft skin. This craving grew and I insisted on going out that evening to visit his married sister. When he wasn't looking, I picked up her kid, fifteen months old and a messy little chap, and stroked his face softly, gently. I stood at the window, hugged him to me and stared at the garden, imagining what it would be like to have a baby of my own. For the first time in my life, I felt what is called the maternal instinct.

"All these cravings and urges that came over me after the abortion were quite bizarre in that they were obsessional in the same way as the eating desires of a pregnant woman are obsessional.

"My husband and I rowed a lot after that, he couldn't understand why I kept on about the abortion and doing the wrong thing and he said I was making myself ill imagining what it would have been like if I had gone on with the pregnancy. In the end he got really mad at me and yelled 'if you feel like that, why did you ever have it done?' Stunned, I looked at him and burst into tears. He had hit the nail on the head, I realised all too clearly that I shouldn't have had it done.

"That night we stopped using contraceptives and nine months later I gave birth to little Sammy. The pregnancy was the unhappiest time of my life. Each month, every twinge, every twitch, reminded me of that previous 'lump of jelly'.

"I thought once Sammy was born I would be able to forget, that he would replace the first one. But it hasn't worked like that. I think about my first baby all the time. On the anniversary this year I left Sammy with my mother for the day, I couldn't bear the hurt of looking at him and remembering.

"I wouldn't say I was at desperation point but my mind is becoming more tormented. I love Sammy dearly, more than my own life and the more I love him the more I remember. Far from fading with time, my pain has grown with time and there is nothing I can do to make amends."

Section 6: The Foreign Scene

The Baby-snatchers

At the time of writing, abortions in the United States of America are permitted up to any stage of pregnancy. There are no rules or restrictions to safeguard the unborn child or mother. Some of the stories related to us, by *pro-abortion* doctors in America and not those from the 'anti' lobby, are a horrifying warning to Britain and the rest of the world of what racketeering and profiteering can besiege a country without stringent legislation in this area of "medicine".

Confirmed reports from American clinics are so harrowing and macabre that it is hard to believe that such inhumanity, butchery and carnage can be tolerated in the "civilised" world. From these satanic stories, one is left wondering, quite seriously, whether there is any hope for mankind.

Gynaecologists who specialise in abortion rather than life-preservation see each pregnant woman as a potential client. Their philosophy is that every pregnant woman should be induced into having an abortion. They do not bother, in America, with any of the sophisticated touting systems of Britain. In America, it is straightforward press-ganging, blackmail, bribery, propaganda, and even force.

Immediately a woman in America discovers that she is pregnant, the battle begins. One side wants her to have the child. The other side wants to kill the baby and make a profit from the abortion. In America, as in Britain, abortion is big business. But, as always, the Americans make things just that bit more brash.

It is not uncommon for abortions to be performed on women who are actually in labour, even when they are "overdue" and are nine and a half months pregnant!

Touts will go into maternity clinics and try to bribe

women, who have gone in to have babies, to have an abortion instead. Whether the women are married or single, it matters not.

Dr. Malcolm Ridley, of Boston, Massachusetts, came to Britain especially to see us. He said that he had been doing "abortion work", but he wanted "out".

"There comes a point in a man's life when he has to take stock, look around, see what he's doing and what others are doing," he explained. "It is only when you stand back from it and observe from the gallery, like a spectator, that you see the truth. What I have seen, I don't like very much, to put it mildly. I'm not very proud of myself, either."

Dr. Ridley poured out his story as if making a confession and unloading himself of a burden of guilt that had been weighing very heavily on his conscience for longer than it had been possible to bear.

He had employed "henchmen" who visited women in maternity clinics. With them, they took contracts, which amounted to selling themselves for an abortion instead of having the baby, the reason for their entering the unit.

"Sometimes my men would have to get the ladies drunk," he said. "They might take a bottle of scotch with them. We had most of the maternity staff paid-off, so my boys would have no intrusion problems from the nurses.

"All they were after was a signature on the contract. It didn't matter a damn how they got that signature. As soon as they had it, I would be called. I would do the operation there and then. It didn't matter whether or not we had the money. If we didn't get the cash in advance, then we would charge so much interest, the exact percentage depending on how long we had to wait for the money. In America, we are not all that worried about debtors, especially if they are married and have roots. You see, we have very effective debt-collectors. People never argue with them...

"I've done abortions on women who have actually been in labour. The contractions have started and the baby is just minutes away from being born naturally. You see, the law in America says that an abortion can be performed right up until the time of birth. I've been into labour wards and taken babies away from mothers while the husbands have been pacing up and down in the corridors outside, wondering whether they are going to have a boy or a girl. While they've been clutching a bunch of flowers and wiping away the nervous sweat, we've been dropping their child into an incinerator.

"This is what we call the result of the abortion mentality. You cease to see the baby as anything other than a raw material. You become conditioned so that the baby becomes inanimate, an article of merchandise to be bartered for, like a precious stone. You just want it and you do anything to ensure that it ends in your possession.

"Of course, we had so many nurses on our payroll and the moment a woman entered the maternity clinic, the propaganda would begin. You know, 'it's a great headache bringing up a child, my dear, it's a terrible chore, very tiresome, not fair on the child, really...' The woman is pressurised like this from the moment she is admitted, and, of course, she is at her most vulnerable peak.

"The woman feels the baby kicking, and, of course, she is very, very big by then, so the nurses in our pay would never talk of it as a living being. It would also be referred to as a rather distasteful object.

"The husbands would go berserk, but I always had enough 'heavies' to cope with that kind of trouble.

"There are two subsidiary rackets being run. One is doing an abortion at a late stage, but keeping the baby alive, although the mother thinks it has been killed. Later, the baby would be sold for adoption and we would pocket the profits. Some of the babies would be flown over to Britain for adoption where there has been an acute shortage of new-born kiddies for adoption because of the Abortion Act.

"The other racket is selling foetuses for experimentation. The babies are officially dead. So they can be kept alive, but are not officially recorded as having been born. Therefore, they can be put to all kinds of experimental use, some of them living for more than a year without being officially born, and being used to test new cures for such diseases as cancer, particularly leukaemia, and in transplant surgery. In the past, animals have been used, but you can never be certain that the treatment will have the same results or be safe on human beings. This is short-circuiting many years of research. Of course, it is morally indefensible.

"In most cases, the babies who were kept alive for experimentation would be 'put down' before they could walk. Now you understand why I want out. The world should wake up to what is happening. The great danger is to believe it is confined to America. Remember, it was the same American money that was used to get the British abortion industry off the ground. The whole push for the 1967 Abortion Act was American-inspired. The money that was thrown about in the 'right' quarters came to a fortune. The big spenders knew they were to retrieve their speculative investments a thousand times."

This doctor's confession was in no way in isolation. Evidence accumulated from nurses, medics and gynaecologists in the abortion field in America, supported everything that had been disclosed by Dr. Ridley.

. . . .

There is an abortion clinic in Amsterdam, Holland, with a business link with one of the biggest "termination" nursing homes in London, England.

We met a nurse who has worked in both clinics. Her story is worthy of reproduction in its virgin state.

"The clinic in Holland is nothing better than a butchery," she said. "The girls are lined up in a row and they have their abortions like that. They hear everything that is happening to the girls in front of them in the queue.

"There is only a flimsy screen between the row of girls waiting and the place where they do the abortions. You've never seen anything like it in your life.

"The doctors and nurses are standing in pools of blood. The walls are splashed with blood. The foetuses, miniature babies, are just dropped from the mother on to the stone floor. The babies are left on the floor and the next girl in the line sees the remains of all the previous butchery.

"It is not until the end of the day that anything is

cleaned up. By then, the whole place is drenched in blood and gore.

"Nearly all the girls are German. This clinic only does abortions up until nine weeks of pregnancy. After that, the girls are transferred to the sister clinic in London.

"The clinic in London employs couriers, who meet the girls at Heathrow Airport or Gatwick. The girls are despatched in batches of fifty. On arrival at an airport in Britain, they are instructed to make their way to the desk of a certain car-hire firm. A fleet of cars are regularly hired from this firm to drive the girls between airports and the clinic.

"This London clinic advertises in books and newspapers abroad. The girls arrive with these advertisements and the clinic officials get very angry and rip them up, because they are not allowed to advertise in this manner. The clinic heirarchy are very sensitive about this kind of thing, because they are terrified of being closed down.

"I've never felt so sick in my life. The doctors stand in the clinic counting money like punters on a racetrack. As soon as the girls arrive, the money is taken off them and shared out among the doctors. They are always over-booking, too. If the Ministry of Health was doing its job properly, this clinic would have been closed down permanently a long, long time ago. It's evil. They do far more abortions in a year than they are licensed to perform, but half the abortion forms are destroyed. This way they are doing twice as many operations as they are supposed to do and are making twice as much profit, because only half of them are recorded. This means half the money is pocketed free of income tax.

"Babies are always crying in the theatre. They do it at any stage of pregnancy. It doesn't matter a damn what the law says. If you can afford it, they will do it. They just manipulate the dates. Who can tell when the baby is dead?

"They change the staff like shirts. We are indoctrinated to avoid attracting attention to the place. They live in perpetual fear of adverse publicity.

"The two men behind the clinic are both dubious businessmen. One of them has already served a long prison sentence for a very serious crime involving explosives and violence. (One of the men, a financier, is well-known by Scotland Yard as a criminal who puts up the money for big "jobs", like bank robberies).

"All the nurses are more or less foreign. One porter was a drug-addict. They employ all the rogues and 'heavy' men for protection. Abortion clinics are part of gangster-land now."

What more is there to add?

Conclusion

Conclusion

It is impossible to run the abortion gauntlet and not emerge the other end with compelling convictions, unless one is utterly insensitive.

One of the most frightening and alarming aspects of all is the fact — admitted by everyone in the abortion industry — that they never really know on whom they are operating. It is expected, almost taken for granted, that the patient is proffering a false name and address. This is never cross-checked in the private sector. The medical record and history of a girl is hardly ever known or seen. Therefore, operations are performed on girls to whom surgery could be dangerous. A girl could die and a surgeon would never know whom he had killed. More important is the fact that a girl returns home after an abortion and, because her family doctor is not informed of the operation, it is never registered on her medical sheet. This means that if she suffers any after-effects — mental or physical — as a result of the abortion, the family doctor or subsequent psychiatrist has no chance of unearthing the root cause, because that is the very item omitted from her records.

A pregnant girl with a modicum of cash does not have to demand an abortion. Her biggest problem is trying to resist having it thrust upon her.

We met taxi-driver touts who worked for abortion agencies. They told of agencies that keep black books containing the names and addresses of foreign girls, mainly French or German, who passed through their hands on the way to the abortion factories.

"Once or twice," said one of the touts, "I had to go to Germany to 'fix' some girls to make sure they did not talk, because there was a bit of a scare on. Some of these agencies run quite a lucrative blackmail business on the

179

side. They never allow the girls to escape their clutches — the foreign ones, that is. You see, abortion is illegal in Germany. If a German girl has an abortion in Britain, she can still be prosecuted when she returns to Germany. So the agency has them under their thumbs for life. They threaten to tell the authorities, or, if she marries, to inform her husband. Some girls pay for ever..."

The Lane Report made the limp suggestion that the time-limit for an abortion should be reduced by a month from twenty-eight weeks to twenty-four. It would make little difference, in our opinion, if the limit was reduced to two weeks. As one "counsellor" said: "We can always fiddle the dates. Who can tell once the only evidence is in the incinerator?"

Of course, it was impossible to take part in research of this nature without it triggering off within us very vital, poignant and pertinent questions on the moral issue. We decided that if it could be proven that the foetus was living, then, morally, abortion was homicide. One cannot compromise or have areas of grey on these kinds of issues.

It is no use talking about a woman's right, if that right is taking the life of another human being, a separate entity. It is no use saying that the foetus is dependent on the mother for life. We are all, whatever our age, dependent on other human beings for life. The two-year-old child cannot live without the support of its mother. The 80-year-old cannot live without the help and support of younger people. Can they be expended? Of course not.

Contraception is the prevention of life being created. Abortion is the deliberate and cold-blooded destruction of life *already* created. The two should never be allowed to fuse into one issue.

The medical world has already defined death as the moment when all brain activity ceases. It is only logical, therefore, that when there is brain activity, there must be life. *And brain activity in the unborn child begins in the second week after conception through the nervous system...*

The trouble, we came to the conclusion, is that the word foetus is so uncommunicative: It is made to appear inanimate. Time and again we heard the foetus referred to as "just a lump of jelly". Far from it: the foetus is another stage in the development of a human being. It should be looked upon no differently from adolescence, middle-age or infancy – all phases of a person's lifespan.

No one says that a child aged two is less human than an adult because so many of its mental and physical faculties have still to mature. Life has never been measured in feet and inches, shapes or sizes. The air is full of life, but no one denies its existence because it is too small to be seen by the naked eye. The point is, that to say the foetus is only a few inches long at a certain stage of pregnancy is as irrelevant as saying that a two-year-old child is only three feet tall, or whatever.

So what?

Once you accept that the unborn baby is living, the argument is clear. Psychologists are adamant that the avid pro-abortionists have fascist tendencies. This was evident from our inquiries and comes out in certain chapters of this book. Selective killing – which abortion is – and selective breeding, were Hitler's brainchildren.

When a woman seeks an abortion, she is hiring a "hit man", a professional killer, who will dismember her baby and dump it in a bucket for a fee, not always a fat one. Even the Mafia have more scruples.

Abortion can thrive only in a climate where women are blinded from the truth. The pro-abortionists realise that they have to talk only in cold facts and figures, and shrink from any emotion. They know that if a woman once knows the baby inside her is alive and looking every part a baby, to assassinate her own flesh is unpalatable.

Of course, women should have as much freedom over their bodies as possible. So should men. But we only allow freedom of one's body as long as it is not encroaching on the freedom of another, providing what we do does not threaten the life of another human being. It is not sufficient for a woman to say that she cannot cope. We do not say that a woman with six children has the right to kill off a couple of them because she is finding it difficult to manage.

The womb is an incubator. Imagine the outrage if a hospital killed a child by switching off the supply to one of their incubators, saying it was their electricity and therefore their right to cut it off at random.

Abortion is the physical ejection of a baby from nature's own incubator. Abortion is also the philosophy of the reactionary, and not the libertine. Finally, abortion is made for man, not woman. Throughout the ages, it has been the men pushing women to the back-street abortionists against their will. Abortion is the vehicle on which man can escape from his responsibilities.

The argument that to repeal the 1967 Abortion Act would send girls rushing to the back-street abortionists is a red-herring. If something is wrong, you do not legalise it to prevent it from happening. You do not legalise bank robberies to bring down the crime figures. The answer is not to legalise abortion, but to be tougher and more determined with the back-street abortionists. Of course, there should still be abortion available for genuine life or death medical reasons. But the iniquitous social clause must go.

When capital punishment existed in Britain, no pregnant woman could be hanged on the grounds that it was immoral to take the life of an innocent party — the child. So the unborn baby has always, in law, been considered a separate and living member of society. Unborn, maybe, but not *unalive*. Here is where so many thoughts on the subject become malformed. The same politicians who found hanging a pregnant woman so repugnant voted for the Abortion Act! The inconsistency and illogicality of man!

Appendices

Appendix A: The 1967 Abortion Act

The 1967 Abortion Act allows the termination of a pregnancy under certain conditions. There are four grounds for which a legal abortion may be authorised. They are:—

1. The continuance of the pregnancy would involve a risk to the life of the pregnant woman greater than if the pregnancy were terminated.

2. The continuance of the pregnancy would involve risk of injury to the physical or mental health of the pregnant woman greater than if the pregnancy were terminated.

3. The continuance of the pregnancy would involve risk of injury to the physical or mental health of the existing child/children of the family of the pregnant woman greater than if the pregnancy were terminated.

4. There is a substantial risk that if the child were born it would suffer from such physical or mental abnormalities as to be seriously handicapped.

Two doctors have to decide, in *good faith*, that an abortion is justified under one or more of the legitimate grounds. Two doctors have to fill in the official green abortion consent form for each patient, signing that their decision is reached in "good faith" and ticking the grounds chosen for consenting — 1, 2, 3 or 4.

No time limit for an abortion is included in the Act. The Infant Life (Preservation) Act 1929, however, is recognised as setting the "ceiling" in this matter. The relevant part of this Act, which does not apply to Scotland, says: "For the purpose of this Act, evidence that a woman had at any material time been pregnant for a period of twenty-eight weeks or more shall be prima facie proof that she was at that time pregnant of a child capable of being born alive."

Appendix B: The Lane Report

In the spring of 1974, the Government-appointed Mrs. Justice Lane Committee, which had been looking into the working of the 1967 Abortion Act for three years, published its findings. There were no surprises. Most shrewd political observers and commentators had forecast a whitewash.

Here are some of the conclusions of the Lane Report:—

"Most women who become 'unwantedly' pregnant suffer some mental disturbance such as distress, anxiety, depression, frustration, hostility or rage, but only in a small percentage of cases does mental illness develop as a result of pregnancy. Where marked emotional disturbance or instability does appear, this has been present in some degree prior to the pregnancy.

"The risk of a serious mental illness, or even of any kind of disabling mental disturbance after a therapeutic abortion appears to be slight. There is, however, a significant number of women who suffer more or less transiently from feelings of depression, bereavement, regret and guilt. A reaction of guilt may be a factor in precipitating a depressive illness in the post-operative period: in the longer term, it may constitute a psychic wound which renders the woman more vulnerable to mental breakdown under stress in later life. Further, feelings of guilt may provoke a young girl or woman into quickly becoming pregnant again in circumstances which may be unchanged or even less favourable.

"According to opinion polls and enquiries, a majority of public and medical staff are still against abortion on demand or request. To expect doctors to work under orders from patients would be contrary to acceptable medical practice.

"There are official statistics which show that proportionately more maternal deaths occur from childbirth than from first-trimester abortion. This is seen by some doctors and others as justifying early abortion in every case in which it is sought. It has been suggested that there is no such thing as an abortion which is illegal for lack of grounds, since the published mortality figures show that early abortion is the lesser risk.

"We do not accept this argument. The statistically established risk must be taken into account, but the decision must be made on the fact and probabilities in the individual case. We regard as wholly unethical the practice, which we have been told exists among a few doctors, of signing without even seeing the patient, in reliance on the statistical argument to justify doing so.

"Prosecution for breaches of the Act, based upon an absence of medical 'opinion formed in good faith' would hardly be rendered any less difficult than it is now if other limiting words were substituted. Accordingly, we do not recommend any relevant amendment of the Act.

"We recommend that the Abortion Act should be amended to authorise abortion up to the twenty-fourth week of pregnancy and not thereafter.

"Some doctors are hard-pressed for time to devote to each patient seeking an abortion and find it easier and quicker to say 'yes' than to say 'no'. We know this happens because we have been told so by some of these doctors themselves.

"BPAS and PAS, with their moderate fees, which may be reduced or remitted in needy cases, provide an excellent service which, so far from being curtailed, should be encouraged and should receive Government support.

"Much of the adverse criticism is justified. It is through the activities of some of these bodies (pregnancy referral agencies and pregnancy advisory bureaux) that a number of scandals in the private sector have arisen. Some of such bodies are run by taxi-drivers or former taxi-drivers. These bodies have been responsible for touting. We have heard of doctors who have availed themselves of these disreputable means of obtaining patients, who are said to have been blackmailed by those who provided them. Further, we regard as undesirable the various fee-splitting arrangements which exist between some doctors and nursing homes or clinics.

"We recommend that all medical referral services should be licensed by the Secretaries of State.

"So great are the profits to be made from the abortion of foreign women coming here for the purpose, that probably some doctors and nursing homes would seek to evade the law (if amendments were made to prevent abuses). Further, even worse scandals and abuses might spring up as a result of competition for the reduced number of non-resident women available as patients. In any event, the abuses in the private sector, with regard to resident women, should not be diminished."

Appendix C: The Wynn Report

In March 1971, the Foundation for Education and Research in Child Bearing was established. It is a registered charitable trust. Its aims are twofold: to disseminate basic information on all aspects of child-bearing to as wide an audience as possible, and to encourage and to assist research in this area of medicine, including foetal life, making known the results by means of papers, lectures and public meetings.

A year later, a report entitled, "Some Consequences of Induced Abortion to Children Born Subsequently", was produced for the Foundation by Margaret and Arthur Wynn. Margaret Wynn is the author of "Fatherless Families" and "Family Policy". Arthur Wynn joined the Government service on leaving Trinity College, Cambridge, and became Chief Scientific Officer. His next appointment was Director of the Safety in Mines Research Establishment, concerned with the prevention of industrial accidents and disease. From 1955 to 1965, he was Scientific Member of the National Coal Board, being responsible for the medical service at Board level. He joined the Ministry of Technology in 1965, retiring in 1971.

Here we list a number of pertinent points made in the Wynn Report:—

The numbers of legal abortions have not been accompanied by any corresponding reduction in illegitimate children.

Abortion is being used increasingly as a contraceptive. There is evidence that more than half the women seeking abortions had not used any method of contraception.

The rising abortion rate seems to be having a rather small effect on the number of pre-marital conceptions carried to term. Unmarried women, unlike married women, are taking

189

less care year by year to avoid conception. Reliance on a more liberal abortion law could be one factor encouraging the trend which may be expressed in the statistical terms that it takes four to five abortions to reduce live births by one.

Large numbers of young women and girls who become pregnant have an abortion believing that it restores them to their physiological and psychological condition preceding the conception. However, the evidence is clear that abortion frequently reduces a woman's future reproductive capability.

There are papers from a number of other countries proving that induced abortion increases perinatal mortality, subsequent spontaneous abortions, subsequent ectopic or extra-uterine pregnancies, the proportion of premature births and a variety of other complications affecting later pregnancies. The substantial increase in the number of premature births to women with a history of abortion is reported from several countries. The overall prematurity rate in Hungary increased from seven percent in 1954 to twelve percent in 1968. Abortion was legalised there in 1956.

An increase in prematurity rates or in perinatal mortality rates is normally accompanied by increasing numbers of children born handicapped. During the six years following the liberalisation of abortion in Japan, the number of births fell by thirty-seven percent, while the infant death rate from congenital malformations rose by forty-three percent. The infant death rate due to congenital malformations was thirty percent higher in 1960 than it had been in 1947. For every congenitally malformed child that dies, there are others less damaged that survive. The cost to the health services and to the community of children born physically or mentally handicapped is one of the main costs of all welfare provisions. Any new measures, like the 1967 Abortion Act, that can be interpreted in practice as to increase the cost in human suffering and money, merit the most careful scrutiny. The complications of subsequent pregnancies resulting in children being born handicapped in greater or less degrees could be the most expensive consequence of abortion for society, and most grievous results for the individual and her family.

The number of abortions aimed at reducing the number of handicapped children is very small compared with the abortions liable to increase the prevalence of handicap.

A man is more likely to have a sterile wife or a stillborn or defective child if he marries a girl who has had an induced abortion.

A Swedish Government report refers to four or five percent sterility following induced abortion. These are high risks by standards generally acceptable in all other spheres of life's hazards. A family will insure its house against fire where the odds are one hundred times better.

It would be wise for young women, their parents and future husbands to assume that induced abortion is neither safe nor simple.